Renew... ...discounted only when the book has at ...estchester Comm...sted by another borro...ember of the Visiting Fac...lities of the ...inal Justice Department and the D... ...re Technology. She has had a private c... ...actice for more than ten years, and conducts special stress workshops for the fire and police departments as well as for people in business and at home. She writes and lectures extensively, and is the author of *The Female Stress Syndrome* (Newmarket Press, New York). She is also consulting editor of the Harper & Row text *The Psychology of Being Human*, and serves on the editorial board of the *Journal of Preventive Psychiatry*. Dr Witkin-Lanoil lives in Westchester County, New York, U.S.A.

Overcoming Common Problems

A successful and popular series to give you practical help for the emotional and medical problems of everyday life.

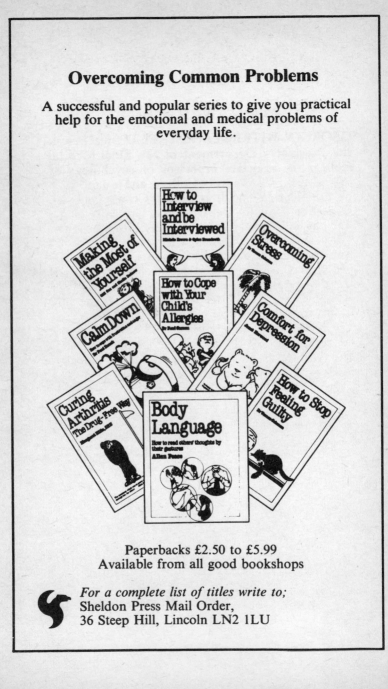

Paperbacks £2.50 to £5.99
Available from all good bookshops

Overcoming Common Problems

COPING WITH STRESS —
A WOMAN'S GUIDE

Georgia Witkin-Lanoil, PhD

SHELDON PRESS
LONDON

First published as *The Female Stress Syndrome* in the
United States of America and Canada in 1984 by
Newmarket Press, New York

First published (revised and abridged edition) in
Great Britain in 1985 by
Sheldon Press, SPCK, Marylebone Road, London NW1 4DU

Third impression 1990

Thanks are due to Pergamon Press Ltd., for permission to
reproduce the Holmes/Rahe Social Readjustment Rating
Scale from the *Journal of Psychosomatic Research*, Vol. II
(1967), 227, pp. 213–218.

British Library Cataloguing in Publication Data

Witkin-Lanoil

Coping with stress.—Rev. and abridged ed.—
(Overcoming common problems).
1. Women—Psychology   2. Stress (Psychology)
I. Title   II. Witkin-Lanoil, Georgia
III. Witkin-Lanoil, Georgia. Female Stress
syndrome   IV. Series
155.9′088042   HQ1206

ISBN 0-85969-438-0

Typeset by Photobooks (Bristol) Ltd.,
Printed in England by Clays Ltd, St Ives plc

Contents

Introduction   1

1. Good Stress, Bad Stress, and Female Stress   6

2. Stress and the Female Body   12

3. Female Stress Symptoms   22

4. Nonassertiveness Training and the Female Stress Syndrome   36

5. Love, Sex and Marriage under Stress   42

6. Mothering and the Female Stress Syndrome   54

7. Stress and the Working Woman   62

8 Hidden Stresses   71

9. Female After Forty   81

10. Living with Female Stress   92

Bibliography   104

Index   105

TO *my mother and father, my loving family and my dear friends.
With special thanks to
Esther Margolis
Larry Abrams
Constance Freeman
Joseph Hankin
Jerry Bucci
Patricia Schreiner-Engel
Raul C. Schiavi
Sharon B. Diamond
Katherine Heintzelman
and my wonderful daughter,
Kimberly Hope*

Introduction

Complete freedom from stress is death.

HANS SELYE

We are warned every day about the potential dangers of stress. We are told that stress can be held responsible for high blood pressure and low blood pressure; for overeating and loss of appetite; for fatigue and for hyperactivity; for talkativeness and for withdrawal; for hot flushes and for cold chills. We are advised that under stress we are more susceptible to infection, depression, accidents, viruses, colds, heart attacks, and even cancer. We worry about the ageing effects of stress and then worry about the effects of worrying! We are stress-conscious and stress-concerned. We are not, however, sufficiently stress-educated.

Our stress education is inadequate because its main focus has been on men and their life-work patterns. Executive pressures, professional expectations, and competitive behaviours have been described by the experts mainly with men in mind. For years newspapers, books, magazines, television documentaries, and lecturers have discussed the serious effects of stress on men—high blood pressure and heart problems, in particular.

But women, after all, live in the same world as men. They, too, get cut off in traffic, hassled at work, and disappointed in love. They, too, worry about their families, become frightened by the future, and are surprised by the present.

Women become depressed, unable to sleep, withdrawn, irritable, childish, frightened, anxious, listless, and distracted under stress, just like men. Under stress, women can lose interest in food, sex, or friends, just like men. Their blood pressure may climb, their heart rate may double, their breathing may become fast and irregular, their hands and feet may become cold and clammy, their mouth may

1

become dry and their digestion may seem to stop altogether
—just like men.

In addition, women experience some stresses all their
own. Men do not menstruate, become pregnant, or go
through menopause. Men do not typically have to justify
their marital status to an employer or their sexual behaviour
to their family. Women must deal continually with society's
mixed messages: they are most often expected to be sexy,
but not sexual; to have a child, but remain childlike; to be
assertive, but not aggressive; to hold a job, but not neglect
their home. Etcetera.

These special, all-female stresses—both physiological
and psychological—result in many symptoms of tension
that are unique to women, and many others that are found
more frequently in women than in men—symptoms
ranging from loss of menstruation to crippling panic
attacks; from fleeting headaches to life-threatening anorexia.
And yet when women complain of these symptoms of
tension and stress, they tend not to be taken as seriously as
men are. Whereas men are given serious tests and
treatment for their ailments, many physicians still prescribe
tranquillizers for women, or tell them, 'Go home and try to
relax. Your problem is just stress.'

'Just stress.' I am always amazed when I hear that phrase.
'Just stress' can trigger or contribute to diabetes, hypertension, and heart attacks. 'Just stress' can trigger or
contribute to depression, anxiety, insomnia, accidents,
alcoholism, and drug abuse; can mimic senility, mental
retardation, hyperactivity, and motor co-ordination problems;
mediates all psychosomatic disorders, including ulcers,
asthma, and allergies. And 'just stress' can bring on the
cluster of psychological and physiological symptoms women
suffer that I call the female stress syndrome.

My awareness of the female stress syndrome did not, as
you might imagine, come from a recognition of my own
stresses and stress symptoms. I was as much a victim of
female stress unawareness as were my female psychotherapy patients. I was a full-time college professor, full-time
psychotherapist, full-time mother, full-time author of text-
books, part-time clinical supervisor, part-time consultant,
semi-efficient housewife, and inefficient bookkeeper.

I was full-time stressed and part-time guilt-ridden. Like most working mothers, I was haunted by a long list of *shoulds*. I *should* be more active in the Parent Teacher Association. I *should* be baking with my daughter on snowy afternoons. I *should* be editing or billing *instead* of baking with my daughter on a snowy afternoon! Like most women, I was concerned with the shape of my body and wardrobe— or the lack thereof. Like most homeowners, I was plagued with put-off repairs and immediate emergencies. Like most people in their middle years, I was worrying about time running faster than I could.

Symptoms? Of course I had symptoms. Headaches, backaches, erratic premenstrual tension, unusual allergies, a touch of colitis. 'Just stress,' my doctor said. 'Just stress,' I reassured myself, and continued on my way.

Ironically, my female stress syndrome awareness was first raised by a man, who was telling me about his daughter. She had a new marriage, new house, new baby, and a full-blown stress syndrome. She was very unhappy, and feeling very guilty about being unhappy. 'I'd be overwhelmed by all that change and responsibility,' he said, 'but *she* thinks that she should be able to do everything and bake bread, too. Please tell her as a psychologist, woman-to-woman, that it's OK for her to feel stressed. That she can sympathize with herself and help herself without feeling guilty or inadequate. No one else is telling her that!' 'Of course I'll speak to her,' I replied; and I began to think about the many stresses that fall primarily on women.

My second consciousness-raising experience followed the next week. I was leading a stress-management work-shop and I gradually realized that the questions and concerns expressed by the women were different than those raised by the men. The women spoke of many more stresses that were long-term and largely beyond their control—the two factors that make stress dangerous to psychological and physical health! They spoke of unequal pay and unequal say. They spoke of double duties: housework and work-work. They spoke of sabotage on the home front: sometimes intentional, but more often not. And they kept adding, 'No one takes me seriously until I am sick in bed for a week'!

Sensitized to this issue of women and stress, then, I went over a decade of therapy notes about female patients. What stresses could women claim as their own? I found many:

- The stresses associated with their *physiology*—breast development, menstruation, pregnancy, and menopause.
- The stresses that can be associated with their *life changes*—becoming a wife, becoming a mother, being female after forty in a youth-beauty culture, becoming a not-so-merry widow, or reorganizing after children have grown.
- The *psychological* stresses often felt by the supposedly swinging single who was raised in an old-fashioned way, the housewife who is pressured to get out of the home and develop herself, the career woman who is pressured to get back into her home lest she lose her family.
- The *hidden stresses* that distract, distress, and deplete—chauvinism, subtle sexism practised by both men and other women, entertaining, and talking to two-year-olds.
- And the stresses of *life crises*, which fall largely on female shoulders—caring for an ill or dying parent, parenting a handicapped child, and making sure that life goes on.

Like the stresses mentioned by the women attending my workshop, these stresses are also long-term and beyond immediate control. Like the women at the workshop, my patients felt the symptoms of stress, but were not taken seriously. Their husbands, doctors, and even their mothers too often said, 'Get a good night's sleep and you'll feel better in the morning.' When they didn't feel better in the morning, they sought a therapist and came to me.

I realized, in time, that the way I was able to help them most was to reassure them that their stresses were not 'all in their minds', but, rather, in their daily lives; that their symptoms were usually not in their imaginations, but, rather, in their bodies. In effect, I gave them the 'permission' they needed to take stress seriously, and encouraged them to educate themselves about their stresses and stress symptoms.

I wrote this book so I could help even more women

educate themselves about female stress and the unique ways in which it affects their lives differently than men's, because of biology and conditioning. I hope this book will also help educate the men who are professionally or personally concerned for the women in their lives.

Unfortunately, many women become expert at identifying and describing their states of tension and symptoms of stress, but don't go beyond that. They find themselves in the same stressful situations again and again. They recognize that they've been there before, but they cannot change their reactions, no matter how upsetting. These women have yet to take the next step, that of stress *management*, which I also emphasize in this book and believe is as important as stress education. To reduce stress and achieve some control over it, we not only need to know and recognize our problems, but we need to gain an understanding of their causes, and learn how to deal with them. I hope this book helps you help yourself live with female stress, so that you can manage it, rather than have it manage you.

ONE

Good Stress, Bad Stress, and Female Stress

Men and women may be created equal, but they are certainly not identical—particularly when it comes to stress. Research continues to uncover fascinating differences between most males and females, some of which are good news for women and their relationship to stress.

For example, females seem to survive birth stress better than males. Not only is the early female mortality rate lower than the male rate, but females usually live longer as well. Women also seem to grow older more gracefully. They tend to retain use of their legs and hands longer, show less grey hair, fewer sight and hearing deficits, and less memory loss, and maintain greater circulation of blood to the brain.

Girls begin to talk earlier and find school subjects such as English and literature easier than boys do. They may also handle stress more logically and verbally than will boys.

Since women typically have a greater fat-to-muscle ratio than men, they have better protection from the cold, better buoyancy in water, and a slower release of energy supply. This helps women cope with long-term stress, since stress tends to constrict the surface blood vessels that keep our hands and feet warm; stress tends to increase sweating, which chills us; and stress tends to suppress appetite, which makes it necessary to have an alternative source of energy.

From Eleanor Maccoby at Stanford University, U.S.A. comes the news that females probably react to touch more easily than males. Perhaps. Might this mean that females' stress can be soothed more easily by holding, hugging, and touching? Probably.

Research also shows a male-female difference in aggression control. After eighteen months of age, girls seem to gain better control over their tempers than boys. This is another reason that females could be expected to evolve better verbal stress-coping strategies than males. They would assess information more efficiently and address problems more logically.

One area of female superiority certainly seems under-utilized: the female's fine-muscle co-ordination. Although this would suit women for occupations such as brain surgery and fine art, in this society it more often results in a woman doing needlework to reduce tension!

Now for the bad news concerning women in relation to stress. Because of their unique physiology and conditioning, women under long-term stress are in a position of double jeopardy: they are at risk for all the usual stress symptoms, from ulcers to hypertension to chronic fatigue, and they are also at risk for such additional stress-mediated disorders as infertility, premenstrual tension, and anxiety neurosis—symptoms that are either unique to women or are more frequently reported by women than men. Before detailing these specific female stress symptoms, though, let's first take a look at the general subject of stress and the ways in which the body reacts to it.

Stress and the General Adaptation Syndrome

Have you noticed how your heart seems to skip a beat or race after a near-accident on the motorway? How about an unexpected encounter with a former lover? In each of these instances, your body is responding to signals from your sympathetic nervous system. It can, for example, increase your heart rate from about 70 beats per minute to 140 beats per minute when you are under stress.

Think about your most recent experience with stress. Since this can involve almost any demand or pressure that induced mental or physical tension, an incident will probably come to mind easily. You may remember being upset, frightened, excited, confused, insulted, elated, aroused, disappointed, annoyed, competitive, saddened, sickened, fatigued, exhausted, or surprised.

Stress can result from something happening around us, or from something happening within. It can result from a work problem, a family crisis, or a bout of self-doubt. It can be caused by factors as diverse as the ageing of our bodies and the birth of a long-awaited child. It can be intermittent, rapid-fire, or chronic.

The primary effect of stress is to mobilize the body's 'fight, flight, or fright' system. This means that stress stimulates the chemical, physical, and psychological changes that prepare us to cope with a threatening situation in these ways.

Suppose, though—as happens all too often in modern life—that the stress you are confronted with does *not* require action. Suppose, for example, that you are late for an important appointment and are held up in bumper-to-bumper traffic. No movement, no escape, and no action. In this situation, relaxation would be of more use than the biochemical and psychological changes created by the fight, flight, or fright system.

Our stress system mobilizes in a similar way to *any* strong demand, whether short-term or long-term; whether it requires action or restricts action; whether it brings good news or bad news. Winning a lottery, for example, stresses the body in much the same way as *losing* a lottery does! Both produce a bodily reaction to stressful situations that involves emergency activation of both the nervous system and the endocrine (hormonal) system.

Within the nervous system, stress messages travel along three pathways. They travel from the brain through motor nerves to arm, leg, and other skeletal muscles, preparing them for motion. They travel from the brain to the autonomic nervous system, which raises blood pressure, heart rate, and blood sugar level; releases reserve red blood cells needed for carrying oxygen to muscles; and slows intestinal movement (since digestion is not a priority in an emergency). And finally, they travel from the brain to the interior of the adrenal gland, which releases adrenaline into the bloodstream as a general stimulant.

The Effects of Short- and Long-Term Stress

If stress is short-term, there is usually no problem, since your body will have time to rest afterward. This occurs naturally when stress is part of a game, a sport, or even romance. The exhilarating feeling you get is 'good stress,' stemming from activities that are stimulating and can be terminated at will.

If, however, the stress is long-term and *beyond your control*, your body will not have a chance to rest. The effects of this 'bad stress' may begin to show. Your heart, after all, is a muscle, not a perpetual-motion machine. Soon you may feel missed beats, rapid beats, a sense of pounding, or even chest pains.

Breathing patterns also change under stress. Breathing becomes more rapid, often doubling its rate, and it also becomes more shallow, like panting. Under 'good' stress these changes are adaptive. Under long-term or 'bad' stress, they create problems. The nose and mouth begin to feel dry from rapid, shallow breathing, and, again, chest pains may develop from working the diaphragm muscles so hard.

Since signals to breathe come from a build-up of carbon dioxide in the bloodstream, rapid, shallow breathing can create another problem: carbon dioxide is expelled *too* well and breathing messages seem to slow down. We feel out of breath and dizzy. This is called hyperventilation, a common symptom of prolonged stress. For quick relief of hyperventilation, you can breathe into and out of a paper bag. In this way, carbon dioxide that has been expelled is breathed into the lungs again, and the carbon dioxide level in the bloodstream is soon high enough to trigger the breathing reflex.

Some psychosomatic effects of 'bad' stress are more difficult to manage. Decreased rhythmic contractions of the digestive system under stress can produce an upset stomach and constipation. The output of certain hormones under stress can gradually increase stomach acidity and, therefore, the risk of a peptic ulcer.

Long-term stress can also produce a *progression* of side effects. The first might be cold hands and feet, then gradually a pale or sallow complexion, and finally migraine headaches or high blood pressure.

As another example, the endocrine glands under long-term stress cause the release of extra sugars for energy into the bloodstream, and extra insulin to break down these sugars for use. If too much insulin is produced, blood sugar levels will become too low. We feel tired and reach for a cigarette, coffee, cola, or sweets to give us a lift. Then even more insulin production is stimulated, and the low-blood-sugar cycle continues.

Look at the following list of stress-related problems. How many have you noticed in yourself? Your family? Your friends?

ulcerative colitis   asthma
peptic ulcer   rheumatoid arthritis
irritable bowel   allergies
heart attack   skin disorders
high blood pressure

Sometimes the symptoms of stress are less serious than these but mimic serious diseases. This, of course, adds further worry to any stressful situation. I often hear patients in the midst of emotional traumas conclude that they have a brain tumour, coronary disease, or cancer, based on some of the stress symptoms listed below.

headaches   dizziness
swallowing difficulties   chest pains
heartburn   backaches
nausea   urinary frequency
stomach 'knots' or   muscle spasms
    'butterflies'   memory impairment
cold sweats   panic attacks
neck aches   constipation
chronic fatigue   diarrhoea
     insomnia

Female Stress

As I noted earlier, women are at risk not only for the ailments listed above but *also* for less well-understood symptoms stemming from their particular physiology, life changes, and the social and psychological demands placed upon them. Most important, the majority of these stresses are long-term and beyond their control—the most dangerous type of stress one can experience. Stress-mediated symptoms that are unique to women include

amenorrhoea (loss of menstruation)	painful intercourse
premenstrual tension/ headaches	frigidity (inhibited sexual arousal)
postnatal depression	anorgasm
menopausal melancholia	infertility

Disorders that are *not* unique to women, but are reported more frequently by them, include

| anorexia | anxiety neurosis |
| bulimia | depressive psychosis |

These are the symptoms of the female stress syndrome, and the sooner we make the connection between their appearance and the incidence of stress in our daily lives—the mind/body connection—the sooner we can help ourselves become healthier. Remember, the stresses and symptoms of the female stress syndrome do not replace, but rather co-exist with, the general stresses and stress symptoms of everyday life. In the next two chapters, we will examine the effects of this double dose of stress on the female body.

11

TWO

Stress and the Female Body

Women are endowed by nature with three complex physiological processes that have no counterpart in men: menstruation, pregnancy, and menopause. These changes are all aspects of a very precious gift, of course—the ability to reproduce—but they can also be both the cause of and the arena for a unique set of stress-related problems. Again, we see how important the mind-body connection is in the development of the female stress syndrome.

The Risk of Premenstrual Tension/Headache Complex

Premenstrual tension is real! During the seven to fourteen days preceding menstruation (and sometimes during or immediately after menstruation), its symptoms can include

headaches
anxiety and nervousness
fatigue
depression and/or
  crying bouts
moodiness (alternating
  highs and lows)
backache and/or pelvic
  pain
fluid retention and
  bloating
food cravings (typically
  sweets, cake, and
  chocolate)
sweating
swelling of the legs
distended stomach with
  or without stomach
  upset
irritability
breast enlargement
  and tenderness
temperature changes
migraine
lowered sex drive
increase in accidents
  and errors
acne, blotching
flaring of allergic
  reactions
outbursts of aggression

It is because these symptoms are so extensive that, until quite recently, many physicians dismissed premenstrual tension as an imaginary condition that gave women a good excuse for not coping with their daily lives. How could such different kinds of symptoms (and seventy-five others not listed) be related?

Nevertheless, research over the past twenty years shows that, indeed, more than half the surveyed female populations in the United States, Britain, and France report psychological and/or physical menstrual changes. In fact, they are probably suffering from different subtypes of premenstrual tension. Katharina Dalton, a British physician who specializes in this area, found links between the premenstrual phase and commission of violent crimes, death from accidents, death from suicide, and admissions to psychiatric hospitals among women, and a correlation between anxiety and the premenstrual phase. Other research shows headaches and a sense of being out of control to be the most frequent symptoms.

Doris's case is not unique. She reports:

> I begin to become short-tempered and irritable as I get closer to my period—irritable in every way. I can't tolerate the noise, the heat, or my children's bickering. I can't even tolerate being touched or stroked. I find excuses to be angry at my family so I can self-righteously go off by myself for a while. Then there is my headache. It comes three days before my period and lasts for two! Aside from eating chocolate and sleeping, the world seems to be empty of pleasure.

Can Doris's problems be explained? Why do headaches develop premenstrually? Why do women become bloated? Tense? Depressed? Why do they become sugar-starved? The triggers are probably within the body. The menstrual cycle is highly complex and powerful, involving the monthly gearing up of the entire reproductive system and its hormones travel in the bloodstream as do the stress hormones, thus reaching every tissue in the body. Also, like the stress hormones, the menstrual hormones set off various chemical reactions and metabolic changes in addition to reaching their target organs.

In the normal cycle, several egg follicles in the ovaries begin growing and secreting the first of the major female hormones, oestrogen.

13

This powerful hormone begins changing the body to prepare for the fertilization of an egg. It causes the cells in the uterine lining to multiply and increases their blood supply. It works changes on the Fallopian tubes and on the uterus, the cervix, and the vagina.

In addition to these changes, oestrogen affects the breasts; the hormones from the thyroid and adrenal glands and the pancreas; the blood vessels; the blood; and bone metabolism.

After nine or ten days, the high oestrogen level in the blood triggers ovulation and a subsequent surge of the second female hormone, progesterone.

Progesterone stops the growth of the uterine lining and further develops it to receive a fertilized egg. Progesterone also begins reversing the changes in the uterus, cervix, and Fallopian tubes.

Although the level of oestrogen has gradually fallen as that of progesterone has risen, on about the twenty-first day of the cycle both are at high levels—and for many women, so is tension. Then if no pregnancy occurs, both hormones are abruptly shut off.

As the uterine lining breaks down and flows out, both hormones are at their lowest ebb. But the lack of progesterone then induces the hypothalamus to again signal the start of a new cycle.

If one part of this cycle is altered, the rest will also be affected. Thus, there are many possibilities for sources of premenstrual tension.

1 There is some evidence that progesterone may be involved, since it is often deficient among women with premenstrual tension/headache complex.
2 When oestrogen is too high or progesterone levels too low in relation to each other, symptoms seem to develop.
3 Since hormone imbalances and diet changes can affect water retention, this area is also being researched.
4 Fluctuations in chemicals involved in brain activity are being examined for sensitivity to oestrogen and progesterone changes.
5 Rather than changes in actual hormone levels, changes

14

in some women's *sensitivity* to hormones may explain premenstrual symptoms.

6 There may be withdrawal reactions to the hormones when they decrease just before the menstrual flow.

7 Changes in the way vitamin B_6 is utilized in the body premenstrually may lead to an increase in a hormone called prolactin. Prolactin in turn can affect fluid retention, causing breast tenderness, swelling, and irritability.

8 Prolactin may also encourage depression, food cravings, and mood swings.

Can stress affect premenstrual tension (PMT) symptoms? Of course. It aggravates the premenstrual symptoms of temperature changes and sweating. It alters tolerance for fatigue, aches, pains, and other people. In other words, premenstrual symptoms will certainly feel worse, and even *be* worse, when a woman is under stress. If she must deal with scepticism about PMT and lack of sympathy as well—more stress!

Fortunately, both medical science and home science have at least partial remedies for PMT. Doctors have recently begun to prescribe antiprostaglandins to counteract premenstrual and menstrual cramping. Tranquillizers can be prescribed for mood changes, but in this case, awareness that mood changes are temporary and follow a premenstrual pattern may be just as effective—without the side effects of tranquillizers.

Home remedies include cutting back on salt intake to reduce water retention (don't overdo this in the summer), heating pads to reduce the discomfort of cramping in the pelvis and/or back, and, under medical supervision, taking low doses of vitamin B_6 daily beginning ten days before menstruation to counteract possible deficiencies. Since PMT can contribute to the female stress syndrome and vice versa, all the self-help and stress-management techniques that are described in later chapters of this book may well make an important difference.

The Stress Risks Involved in Pregnancy

Pregnancy means change, and the stress of change often brings on female stress symptoms. If you are a mother, think of all that changed for you during pregnancy. Most obvious, of course, was the change in your body and perhaps your assessment of your attractiveness. Your health-care responsibilities broadened and alcohol, nicotine, and medication intake had to be monitored.

Your activity level probably changed as a result of morning sickness, which 70 per cent of women experience. If your mate told you that your morning sickness was 'in your head' and you *knew* that it was in your stomach, further stress was obviously added to an already unhappy situation. Your activity level may have slowed even more as your size and weight increased, but soon after delivery you came to suspect that you might never have a moment to sit still again.

Remember, too, how many financial changes were taking place: perhaps the end of your wage-earning for a while, or the beginning of life insurance and saving deposits. And these expenses were just the beginning!

Women often find that their time frame changes during pregnancy. All plans become focused on the due date, and all experiences are remembered as being far from, or close to, delivery. Many women do not have clear plans or expectations beyond that date.

Women may have studied reproduction in biology class, genetics and conception, natural childbirth methods, gentle birth, and neonatal care in maternity classes—but most have never studied mothering. Expectations of motherhood are often no closer to reality than a cartoon is to life; the demands and disappointments this can lead to contribute to the female stress syndrome.

Pre-motherhood
Pre-motherhood is a psychological period, not a time period. It may begin before conception, during pregnancy, or even after the onset of labour! Tension can build, drain energy from happy anticipation, and aggravate postnatal female stress syndrome symptoms.

The cases of Sarah, Edna, and Sandy reflect some of the stresses that can be associated with conception.

> Sarah had been working as a production assistant in an advertising agency, dating Ray, and feeling good about her self-directed life-style. Although she stated that in principle birth control was the responsibility of both members of a couple, she preferred the sexual spontaneity that an intra-uterine device gave her to the 'clumsiness' of a condom. Since she had, therefore, taken on the responsibility of contraception, she was particularly stressed when she accidentally conceived. Although she decided that she wanted the child, she found that she was upset about having lost control over this area of her life decisions, resentful of the changes that were coming, and guilty about her resentment.

For Sarah, therefore, her pregnancy represented both a wish and a fear, and such ambivalent feelings are always associated with some degree of discomfort or stress.

> Although Edna's pregnancy was unplanned, it was a welcome surprise. Edna had worried that she and her husband were not ready for parenthood and the responsibilities of a family. She also suspected, however, that they might never feel ready to make a conscious decision about having a baby, and might delay such a decision far too long. So she put her concerns aside, and prepared for delivery with great excitement. As the time for delivery loomed, however, the realities of parenthood began to frighten Edna and her husband. They became irritable with each other, and each began to see the other as responsible for their plight.

For Edna, stress had begun to build as she approached delivery. She felt that she no longer had a choice about parenting, and that she had betrayed herself by leaving the conception of her child to chance.

> Sandy pondered the considerations of timing, finances, and emotional readiness before she and her husband tried to conceive a child. When the situation seemed right, Sandy was ready. Unfortunately, almost 15 per cent of all pregnancies end in miscarriage or spontaneous abortion before the eighth week, and this was Sandy's experience. Following her mis-

carriage, Sandy's efforts to conceive again were unsuccessful for many months. By the time she did conceive, her anxiety level was high and her focus on motherhood was all-consuming. Even her relationship to her husband was over-shadowed by the prospect of the mother-child relationship to come.

Fear and unrealistic expectations combined to produce a high level of stress for Sandy during her pregnancy. Again, motherhood stress began during pre-motherhood.

Sandy, Edna, and Sarah are by no means unusual cases—their stories are representative of many women's. Pre-motherhood concerns are a very real part of the female stress syndrome. A generalized anxiety about the demands that are made on mothers, fear of miscarriage, of having a defective baby, of labour pain, or even of delivery procedures or Caesarian section.

Postnatal Depression
Depending on the particular study you read, between 20 and 65 per cent of childbearing women report maternity blues. Since depression rarely begins before the third day after delivery, it seems clear that hormonal and chemical changes are involved. But psychological stresses also play an important role.

Stressful changes begin with delivery. The woman is separated from her husband and family except during visiting hours. She is often separated from her baby except during feeding hours. Soon the new mother feels isolated, vulnerable, and incapacitated. Her first days at home with the baby can make things worse. Mary remembers:

> I was totally prepared for natural childbirth, and totally unprepared for natural child-rearing. Despite my twenty years of formal education, I did not know how to sterilize a bottle without melting the rubber nipples. By the end of the week, every time my baby cried, I cried, too.

Teenage mothers struggle with further stresses after delivery: loss of freedom, of mobility, and of choice, and mixed feelings about parenting and its responsibilities.

Some women don't feel the baby blues until they have

their second or third child. As Dora, who has four children, put it, 'It is hard to see myself as pretty, witty, and wise, when I feel more like the old woman who lived in a shoe, and had so many children that she didn't know what to do!'

The postnatal depression should lift as the new mother rejoins her support system, sees that she can handle things, and finds that her body chemistry readjusts. Sometimes it does not. Professional intervention may be necessary to break the mind-body chain of events producing, in this case, the depression.

The Stress Risks Involved in Menopause

Even the most sceptical of physicians and mates usually view menopausal depression as 'real.' That is, they assume *physiological* changes within the woman can explain mood and behaviour changes. She is more likely to receive sympathy and understanding at this time than when she is premenstrual or going through a postnatal depression.

Who can argue with the reality of hot flushes? Who can argue with the reality of the permanent cessation of menstruation? Doctors and husbands understand that menopause represents a landmark along the road to ageing. Who can argue with the assumption that a woman will be depressed at the notion of ageing? Who can argue with the idea that the loss of fertility makes a woman naturally defensive and irritable? Who can argue with the belief that when a woman feels older her sex drive decreases? Researchers can—and do.

It is ironic that much of this sympathy is unnecessary and may even be unhealthy: unnecessary because the most recent research points out that most women do *not* experience increased depression or any other type of mental illness during menopause; unhealthy because such sympathy may encourage women to feel defensive and devalued by assuming that they *should* feel that way during and after menopause.

The happy truth is that many women find the freedom from fear of pregnancy liberating, both sexually and practically. With menopause comes a rite of passage into a period of personal choice and self-defined life-styles—free

19

from premenstrual tension and postnatal blues, free from preparental anxiety, and filled with postparental relaxation. Of course, this is not to say that menopause is always a time free from sadness and stress. Even in women who look forward to their life changes, there may be nostalgia for earlier times, a sense of loss of their ability to have children, and an anxiety associated with entering a later stage of life. Furthermore, menopause is a time for major physical change. Life change and physical change interact, once again. Female stress symptoms can appear, once again.

Physical Changes
Menopause affects nearly every organ in the body.

It begins gradually as the number of egg-containing follicles in the ovaries is reduced, so that the amount of oestrogen produced falls below normal levels. Eventually the delicate hormonal feedback system is disrupted. When so little oestrogen is produced that the uterine lining does not build up enough to flow at all, menstruation ceases.

Not surprisingly, the withdrawal of oestrogen and progesterone from tissues that had been flooded with them monthly has its effects. Blood chemistry and blood vessels must adjust to the change, causing the hot flushes that are experienced by two-thirds of menopausal women. The vaginal and urinary tract tissues tend to become dry and thin and thus more vulnerable to infections. Sometimes painful intercourse and urinary problems result.

Bone metabolism loses an important support with the withdrawal of oestrogen and progesterone. Everyone, including men, loses bone mass with ageing, but post-menopausal women lose it at a higher-than-normal rate. In fact, bones made brittle by loss of minerals—will probably occur in about 40 per cent of all women.

Finally, some women do experience anxiety and depression that seem to be related to the reduction of hormone levels. Many times of body change are times of stress, because we may feel our sense of control threatened. This may increase anxiety and make many women feel helpless or victimized by their bodies.

Marilyn had always exercised, dieted, and maintained a youthful style of dress. She felt that her appearance and health were in her own hands and that her self-discipline was the secret of her 'staying power.' Although she thought that she had accepted the inevitability of menopause, she found that when menopausal changes began, her sense of control was threatened. She looked for, and of course found, every new wrinkle and age spot that appeared. She could no longer predict the rate of her body's changes, and her stress level rose. Feeling that she was fighting a losing battle, she lost her interest in dieting, exercise, and dressing attractively. She became increasingly depressed.

Does Marilyn's story sound familiar? Although the menopausal symptoms themselves may not be under full control, other areas of functioning are. Unlike Marilyn, women who maintain control of their weight, their exercise, and their time can help themselves reduce that feeling of being overwhelmed by inevitable physical changes. Take appropriate control over every area that you can while you are menopausal, and see Chapter 9 for more on the management of menopausal stress.

Depression and stress are not exclusive to changes in body state such as menstruation, pregnancy, and menopause. In fact, often these feelings coincide with body changes only because both come at the same time of life, not because one has been *caused* by the other. For example, a husband's retirement, a daughter's failing marriage, or the loss of one's own parent may trigger a depression mistakenly labelled 'menopausal melancholia.' The loss of one's office friends or autonomy may coincide with the postnatal period. To understand the female stress syndrome fully, we must look in the next chapter at stresses not associated with pre-programmed body changes, and at the body changes that go along with these stresses.

THREE

Female Stress Symptoms

Some of these symptoms of stress are common; some are less so. Some are unique to women; some are simply found more frequently in women than in men. Some involve a physical predisposition; others do not.

Anorexia Nervosa

Donna cuts her food into many little pieces and moves them around her plate. She drinks her coffee and eats the lettuce in her salad, but will not swallow the meat she has put in her mouth. She coughs into her napkin to remove it. Donna is twenty years old, five feet four inches tall, and weighs eighty-seven pounds. Although she has abundant energy for physical activities, within two weeks her malnutrition will endanger her life. Even then she will not seek help voluntarily. She feels fat and wants no interference with her dieting.

Donna's condition is called anorexia nervosa, and it is one of the many stress-related symptoms that are more frequently found among women than among men.

Under the stress of increasingly adult responsibilities, sexual anxiety, or self-conscious concern about their appearance, young women may begin to control their eating and thereby gain a sense of control over their other impulses as well. Soon their appetite is altered, but their body image is not. As young women like Donna become more and more emaciated, their self-image lags behind, and they continue to see themselves as needing to diet.

Why is this disorder so much more common among women than among men? The answer is not clear, but it probably involves female physiology. Appetite changes often accompany the menstrual cycle, for example. Pre-menstrual cravings for sugars, chocolate, and rich or spicy foods are common. The food preferences that accompany pregnancy are legendary. (Pickles and ice cream, anyone?)

Cultural messages probably also encourage women to manage stress through anorexia.

> Cindy was the oldest of many children and felt like a surrogate mother to her brothers and sisters. A little more was always expected of her, and she tried her best to live up to all expectations. Her grades were excellent, her friends were 'nice,' and her family was proud. By the time she was fifteen Cindy was anorexic.

If Cindy is thought of as having 'swallowed' others' demands all her life, the stage is set for her not 'swallowing' any more. By late adolescence, she was facing additional adult responsibilities. Not the openly defiant type to begin with, Cindy took control over herself in this passive way. Her rebellion was symbolic.

> Theresa seemed to be using her anorexia to manage sexual anxieties. She actually delayed her own sexual development by keeping her body thin and childlike. Since her fat/muscle ratio was altered by dieting, even her menstruation was delayed. She dispelled her guilt over sexual impulses by denying her 'appetites,' and her fantasy fear of pregnancy was dispelled by a perpetually flat belly.

Although her mother thought Theresa would be tired from her constant dieting, she found instead that her daughter was overactive. Psychologists would suspect that Theresa's hyperactivity was yet one more attempt to manage unacceptable impulses, by keeping very busy.

There is no mystery as to how anorexia nervosa reflects an obsessional concern with appearance. Anorexics are often 'approval junkies,' trying to live on love and acceptance rather than food. If thin is in, they will want to be the thinnest. They will avoid being fat at all costs: by starvation, vomiting, enemas, and diuretics, to name a few.

At what point should family members worry about a dieting young woman? As soon as they see her dieting excessively without medical supervision, becoming obsessed with fasts, water diets, or fad-food diets. As soon as they suspect her body image is unrealistic. As soon as dieting interferes with her normal menstrual cycle. As soon as they find evidence of her using forced vomiting, enemas, or diuretics to control weight gain. Psychotherapy, family therapy, group therapy, and even hypnotherapy can all help if the problem is treated early enough. If allowed to become severe, anorexia is life-threatening.

Bulimia

How many women are thinking that they would gladly trade in their compulsive eating for a 'mild case' of anorexia? Undoubtedly more women feed themselves than starve themselves when they are under stress. They chomp, chew, and sip, trying to sweeten up, spice up, or fill up their lives.

When gorging and bingeing become extreme and compulsive, the resulting stress symptom is called bulimia. Food can be tied to a memory of being mothered. It can provide a touch of home. It can be a reward, or it can be part of an attempt to gain strength and fortification. It can be a substitute for 'taking in' sexual pleasure, praise, or love from others. It can be a safe outlet for anger: we can chew it, bite it, or cut it. It can be a safe outlet for dependency needs: we can hide it, stock it, and hoard it. The list may go on and on, but the symptom remains the same—uncontrolled eating.

> Gloria binged secretly. Publicly she complained that her sluggish metabolism was responsible for her weight. Privately, she used her obesity as an excuse for her lack of popularity. She periodically tried to diet, but felt too deprived to continue for long. When she was tense, she could imagine no other release, and told herself that her eating was a combination of a bad habit and good cooking.

Gloria was a food addict, and management of her symptom would be a lifelong problem. First she would have to recognize that she was no longer a helpless infant whose only active capacity for soothing herself was to put something in her mouth. She would have to understand that when she had finished her munching, the source of her stress had still not been dealt with. She would have to admit to bulimia. The stress triggers would have to be identified and alternative strategies for coping developed.

Bulimics run many of the same health risks as anorexics. Their diet becomes nutritionally unbalanced as they 'just pick' at healthful foods to compensate for devouring desserts or junk food. Their biochemical balance becomes threatened if they use forced vomiting, enemas, and/or diuretics to undo their loss of eating control. If they hide their bulimia by maintaining normal weight, the disorder is harder to identify and help is less likely to be offered. If they alternate between anorexia and bulimia, they are in double jeopardy.

Alcoholism

Statistics tell us that male alcoholics greatly outnumber female alcoholics, in fact, the ratio is changing. As greater numbers of women are working outside the home, their alcohol problems are becoming more obvious. As women deal with the stresses of what used to be a 'man's world,' their alcohol problems increase. Not surprisingly, so do those of housewives who feel less and less support for their chosen role. More and more, women are seeking treatment for drinking problems. So, while alcoholism is not a distinctively female stress symptom, it is an important potential response to stress.

Alcohol can act as both a sedative and a disinhibitor. Both functions can temporarily reduce a sense of stress. As a sedative, alcohol works like a liquid barbiturate. At low levels it slows muscle response and induces a feeling of relaxation. As a disinhibitor, it affects the brain centre for emotional behaviour and allows the drinker to act out impulses with less guilt. The effect will vary depending upon which of the drinker's impulses are more guilt-associated. If, for example, it is your aggressive impulses that make you feel most guilty and stressed, a few cocktails may transform you into a woman who speaks her mind without hesitation. A few more and you may be speaking without consideration, forethought, or discretion, as well. If, on the other hand, it is your sexual impulses that are ordinarily repressed, you might find yourself dancing on the piano after a few drinks.

The problem with this elixir of relaxation and dis-inhibition is that since the effects of alcohol are achieved by altering judgment, alcohol abuse is difficult to avoid. If one drink makes us feel good, we reason, two drinks will make us feel better. Actually, as alcohol consumption increases, motor co-ordination is impaired, drowsiness progresses into drunkenness, and memory is diminished. We eventually sleep, but dreaming is suppressed and our intestines are affected. The day after is rarely worth the night before. Stresses have not been altered, and our capacity to deal with them has been lowered.

At what point does alcohol use become alcohol abuse? The following brief summary is drawn from the definitions set forth by the World Health Organization and Alcoholics Anonymous.

1 Frequent intoxication or drunkenness (four times per year or more).
2 Habitual use (drinks at dinner having an effect more than once a week).
3 Compulsive drinking (without real choice or control, or out of fear of not being armed with a drink).
4 Addiction (characterized by withdrawal symptoms, such as tremors, seizures, disorientation, or hallucinations).
5 Vocational, social, or physical impairment related to alcohol consumption.

When signs like these are present, the drinker is confronted with two problems: the original stresses and the alcohol abuse they have triggered. Both problems must be treated, and professional help is usually vital. Group therapy, family therapy, or individual therapy, with a trained psychiatrist, psychologist, social worker, nurse, or Alcoholics Anonymous leader all seem to work if the patient is motivated and the therapist is supportive and caring.

Headaches

If headache jokes were fact, it would seem that migraines occur exclusively among long-married women when they are approached sexually by their husbands. Although this is not true, migraines *are* more frequently a female than a male stress symptom. The question is, why?

It would seem that there is a predisposition to react to stress in this way built in to the female physiology. Glands, various blood vessels, and scalp muscles may, under the influence of some female hormones, be particularly susceptible to stress triggers. Blood vessels that narrow in reaction to stress may eventually widen painfully. The walls of the vessels are now irritated and the blood pulsing through feels like pounding pain. This type of headache is a true migraine. Prolonged contraction of the muscles of the face, neck, and scalp produces what is generally called a tension headache. And, finally, secretions from various glands to raise energy levels under stress can also change fluid retention causing yet a third type of headache.

Although fast relief from headache pain is offered in myriad television commercials, relief from the stresses that cause migraine headaches is even better.

> Rosemary knew that her migraine attacks always followed situations in which she was enraged but felt that she couldn't express her anger and feared that showing her anger would destroy her image as the patient wife and mother. She was, in fact, quite sure that her husband would stop loving her if he knew how often she felt irritable and annoyed at being taken for granted.

Imagine Rosemary's surprise when she began to request some appreciation from her family and got it! Her headaches gradually subsided, and she learned that her stress trigger had been an automatic fear of her own angry impulses. Other women have found that their dependency needs or sexual interests create similar conflicts and activate their headaches.

If the 'unacceptable' impulse can't be identified or avoided, migraine may warrant a preventive medication.

Amenorrhoea

If a girl has not started to menstruate by eighteen years of age, the diagnosis is 'primary amenorrhoea.' If, however, there has been menstruation and it stops, the condition is called 'secondary amenorrhoea.' Although both types of amenorrhoea can be related to organic problems, stress is the most frequent cause of secondary amenorrhoea.

The mind-body chain of events works like this: stress is perceived and messages are sent through the nervous system to activate the fight, flight, or fright emergency systems. Since the reproductive system is not an emergency support system, its hormone levels are lowered and menstruation is not triggered.

Imagine this: A sexual encounter has caused Sally great anxiety, fear, and guilt. She is distraught at the notion that she may have become pregnant. She worries and worries and waits breathlessly for her period. Her period is delayed by her stress, and her anxiety increases. The scene is set for temporary amenorrhoea.

Imagine this: Carol has decided to transform herself into a facsimile of a *Vogue* model. She begins to diet drastically. She eliminates desserts. Then breads. Then fats. Then sweets. Her menus have been stripped down and *she* has been stripped down to skin and bones. She has lost her stomach, her hips, her waist, and her period. Amenorrhoea!

Imagine this: It is Lissa's last summer before university. This is her last chance to see if she wants an academic life or the life of a professional dancer. She joins a semi-professional troupe and starts a round of classes at 6 a.m., rehearsals at 1 p.m., and performances at 7 p.m. She makes more and more demands on her body and is proud of its response. She gains a pirouette and loses a period—then another, and another. Again, amenorrhoea.

Imagine the many other stressful situations that can also lead to amenorrhoea. Depression, prolonged grief, and unrelieved anxiety can produce the same effects. Although mature women do not typically lose their periods, the menstrual cycles of young women are more vulnerable. In fact, young anorexics are frequently non-menstruating.

What can be done about amenorrhoea? Relief from the stress is often enough, although sometimes a normal cycle returns even while the stress continues.

Sometimes this does not happen, however. When stress-triggered amenorrhoea continues and a normal cycle does not spontaneously reoccur, a doctor should be consulted. Although the problem may not have started with an organic condition, chronic stress may lead to one. The physician may suggest therapy based on hormones or drugs, or he may suggest psychotherapy instead. Psychotherapy can help patients deal with the immediate stress causing the amenorrhoea and helps to eliminate the risk of future stress symptoms by encouraging the development of more effective coping strategies for the future.

Menstruation and Society's Mixed Messages

For many women, sexual stress reflects negative associations with female body functions. It is women alone who menstruate, gestate, and lactate. They should feel unique, special, and proud. Instead, they often feel embarrassed, inconvenienced, and inferior. Why?

A look at some common taboos shows how women get the message that being female is a physically and psychologically unhealthy state of being.

- Don't swim during menstruation.
- Don't wash your hair during menstruation, because you will get sick.
- Don't handle flowers during menstruation, because they will wilt.
- Don't have your hair permed during menstruation, because it will not take.
- Don't have intercourse during menstruation.

Menstruation is particularly singled out for negative attitudes. Just when a young woman is trying to cope with the stresses of adolescence, she begins to menstruate. In some cultures, this is a cause for celebration. In our culture, it must be kept a secret.

Jennifer's first menstruation started while she was at school. At first, she was frightened when she noticed red stains on her underclothes when she was changing for gym. She was twelve and had no sex education at school. Her mother had never spoken to her about menstruation—or about anything else that personal, either. Jennifer had never allowed herself to think about 'that part' of her body, nor look at her genitals with a mirror. She had only a vague notion of her sexual anatomy.

Jennifer had heard from the boys on her school bus that the first 'period' was the bloodiest. Her fear turned to worry. She didn't dare go to gym, leave the locker room, or even get up off the bench. She was trapped. She wondered when the cramps and headaches she had heard about would start. She was still sitting on the bench, frozen by her anxiety and confusion, when she was rescued by a teacher.

Advertisements for tampons and sanitary towels emphasize the need to hide any signs of menstruation, avoid any possibility of an 'accident,' and forgo adjusting one's activities in any way. 'No one but you will know,' they seem to be saying.

Like Jennifer, many adolescents worry about hiding their secret month after month. They feel odd if they start menstruating early in puberty, they feel odd if they start late, and they feel odd *while* they are menstruating. It's certainly not hard to understand how females can develop negative feelings about a body function referred to as the curse, being unwell and that time of the month.

It is but a short step to developing self-conscious sexual inhibitions.

Frigidity—Inhibited Sexual Arousal

The term 'frigid' is outdated, although it used to be quite commonly used. It conjured up images of unfeeling, uncaring, icy-cold women who were rigidly unresponsive to demonstrations of physical affection. In fact, the label was meant to describe a sexual dysfunction in which stress interfered with the swelling and lubrication of the female genitals in response to sexual stimulation—a problem that is now called inhibited sexual arousal.

Does this inhibited response mean the woman has no interest in sex or physical affection? Absolutely not! Often she enjoys the contact and is unaware on a conscious level of the source of her fight, flight, or fright reaction.

Rhonda had looked forward to her honeymoon as a time of romance and privacy. She had lived at home until her marriage and had 'saved herself' for her husband. When the time for lovemaking finally arrived, Rhonda found that 'nothing happened.' She liked being close with her husband, but couldn't share his sexual excitement. He, in turn, felt like a sexual failure, and soon the stress level climbed.

In sex therapy, Rhonda's stress was traced to her self-conscious fears of loss of control. She was concerned about what reactions were 'normal.' She was so busy worrying that she could not stop watching herself and abandon herself to the pleasure of the experience with her husband. Learning that flushing, nipple erections, rapid breathing, and utterances are all common relieved her stress.

Vaginismus

Another less common stress-related sexual problem is vaginismus. Women with vaginismus would like to achieve normal sexual intercourse, but involuntary contraction of the muscles surrounding the vagina makes penetration painful or impossible.

Flora told her doctor that she thought she had no vaginal opening. Although she had never examined herself with a mirror, she could not feel an orifice with her finger nor insert a tampon. Her doctor attempted a pelvic exam, but found that although her vulva was normal, Flora's involuntary muscular contractions were so strong that she could not be dilated for an internal examination.

A number of stresses can be responsible for vaginismus, including fear of pain, fear of pregnancy, fear of intimacy, fear of punishment, fear of intrusion, fear of 'contamination,' fear of dependency, and fear of rape. Vaginismus is, in fact, very often the product of an early rape—by a stranger, boyfriend, husband, or even family member. The contractions that were meant to protect the victim from the stress of unwanted intercourse can remain and prevent desired intercourse.

In cases such as this, both the symptom and the stress need treatment. Gradual dilation and accommodation of the vagina to the patient's own fingers, can be made in the privacy of her own home. If the inhibition seems unyielding, trained sex therapists can help deal with the underlying fear and stress.

Orgasm Problems

Perhaps the most common sexual stress symptom among women is orgasmic dysfunction.

- Five to 15 per cent of the female population surveyed reports never having achieved an orgasm. This is called primary orgasmic dysfunction. Most researchers associate this condition with the stress created by guilt. Sexually repressive backgrounds seem common among those who suffer from it.
- Forty-five to 60 per cent of the female population surveyed reports having difficulty achieving orgasm at certain times or with certain partners. This is called situational or secondary orgasmic dysfunction, and is usually related to lack of sexual arousal due to the stress of fights or fears. An orgasm requires an autonomic 'letting go' and giving up of control; fights and fears, on the other hand, require 'holding on' and a struggle *for* control.

There are many other stresses that can inhibit orgasm. Fear of punishment, fear of criticism, fear of abandonment, concern with appearing aggressive or selfish, reluctance to give a partner the power of pleasure, anxiety about religious taboos, misinformation, guilt, anger, and control issues can all raise female stress levels and inhibit the orgasmic response.

Success rates for the treatment of both primary and secondary orgasmic dysfunctions are usually reported to be as high as 80 per cent.

Infertility

The Lerners were anxious to begin a family and tried without success for at least one year. Diagnosed as functionally infertile, Mrs Lerner became more and more frustrated. She began to feel inadequate and helpless. She turned to the experts, but no organic problems could be found. An adoption seemed to be the next logical step. It restored her sense of decision. It provided her with a new focus of activity. It was a goal that she and her husband could share.

The Lerners did, in fact, adopt a girl and begin to parent together. Within the year, Mrs Lerner became pregnant.

Most psychologists know couples like the Lerners. How do they explain a case in which the woman seems infertile, though no organic reason presents itself, until *after* she has adopted a child? The answer can lie in the female stress syndrome. Fears and conflicts about mothering can produce stress, which in turn interrupts and alters hormonal functioning, which in turn affects ovulation, which in turn provides a solution to the conflict—no pregnancy. After hidden and unconscious fears are dispelled by parenting the adopted baby, stress is reduced, endocrine functioning returns to normal, and conception is more likely.

Anxiety Reactions

Sylvia was waiting for a bus at the end of a hot summer day. The buses were full and a crowd of commuters swarmed around her. As bus after bus passed them by, Sylvia began to wonder if she would ever get home. She also began to wonder why her breathing was so very shallow and rapid. She felt as though her breathing might stop altogether. Her palms were both cold and clammy, and although the air was muggy she was now shivering slightly. More alarmed than bewildered, she started walking home rather than waiting a minute longer for a less-crowded bus. As she half-ran, half-walked, panic welled up. Her heart pounded and she feared that she would not make it home. Terror seemed to come in waves, each leaving her more exhausted than the last. She reached her door, but her hands were shaking so violently she could not use her keys. She stood by her door, desperate. Within minutes, however, the panic subsided, and she entered her home shaken and mystified.

Sylvia was suffering from a panic attack. Her fight, flight, or fright reaction seemed to come from nowhere. As in the case of Rosemary's headaches, the stress triggering Sylvia's reaction was also an internal conflict between a wish and a fear. Sylvia wished to break loose at the end of her work day but also feared that impulse. With professional help she came to accept her impulse and handle it realistically—and her panic attacks subsided.

The female-to-male ratio for anxiety disorders is a disturbing three to two. The reason for this is unclear, but part of it may lie in the way girls are raised in our society. According to research, fathers emphasize achievement, self-assertion, aggressiveness, and self-aggrandizement in their sons, but expect their daughters to control these same qualities. Is it any wonder that women think of many of their impulses as 'dangerous'? Is it any wonder that women see themselves as more fragile and vulnerable than men?

Anxiety attacks are best treated by professionals—psychiatrists, psychologists, and psychiatric social workers. Before, during, and after treatment, however, support systems are vital. So too is knowledge of crisis-intervention procedures, which can help until a professional is found. Read about these procedures in the last chapter of this book, and help others help themselves.

Weak Links and Other Theories

How is it, you may be wondering, that a particular woman develops a particular stress symptom at a particular time?

One theory is that anxiety and stress aggravate problems that already exist because of our genes, prenatal environment, diet, or earlier diseases, damage, or accidents—symptoms waiting to happen.

Another, similar, theory is that each organ and system has lowered resistance levels when the body is subjected to a high degree of anxiety or stress. When this happens, a virus, disease, or disorder is more likely to appear. Historically, many theories have tried to associate certain stress symptoms with certain personality profiles. Even Sigmund Freud agreed with this approach. In fact, he thought that both a particular personality profile and a particular stress

34

symptom resulted from the same early childhood experiences. A woman with unfulfilled dependency needs, for example, might show more eating and gastrointestinal disorders than is usual, whereas a woman who has difficulty expressing her anger directly might have a tendency to develop sexual dysfunctions.

Many theories about why women develop the symptoms that they do focus on the importance of individual differences among women under stress. It is as if each has her own threshold for psychosomatic reactions, and her own combination of variables that can push her over that threshold.

- The *amount* of stress needed before a symptom is produced can vary.
- The *number of times* the same or similar stress is experienced may affect women differently.
- The *physical condition* of each woman, and her *emotional state* preceding and during exposure to a stressful situation may influence her threshold.
- The significance of *age* to stress symptoms varies from woman to woman, as does the *readiness* to cope or capitulate.

Every one of these theories attempts to explain why a specific stress symptom appears in a particular woman at a particular time. It is most likely, however, that the factors mentioned are *interacting* to produce the various stress symptoms. In the next chapter, we will look at the world into which girls are born and see how the groundwork is laid for future stress patterns.

FOUR

Nonassertiveness Training and the Female Stress Syndrome

It's true that every child is a unique individual. It's true that any individual boy can be calm, quiet, and cuddly, and that any individual girl can be active, acrobatic, and athletic. It's true that people—including baby nurses—cannot accurately guess the sex of a baby when it is wrapped in a yellow blanket. It is also true, however, that raising girls and raising boys is different. Ask any parent! Most will tell you that their experience suggests the following.

- Girls are more compliant than boys—more likely to run errands and help out.
- Girls seem more social and concerned with their appearance.
- Girls, although not passive, seem less aggressive than boys.
- Girls show more anxiety than boys.
- Girls use their intuition more.
- Girls speak and read earlier than boys.
- Girls are more emotional and more responsive to emotions.
- Girls have better fine-motor co-ordination.

Most parents will also tell you that boys are a handful because

- Boys are more active than girls tend to be.
- Boys stay awake longer.
- Boys take everything apart.
- Boys are harder to keep track of, will roam farther and more often.
- Boys lose their tempers more easily than girls.
- Boys prefer more action and violence and less talking than girls, in books, films, and TV.
- Boys engage in more mock fighting and attacks.

Are boys more mechanical than girls, or is it that their curiosity is channelled into dismantling and reconstructing, while girls' curiosity is not? Are boys more aggressive, or is it that their activity level is channelled into contact sports while girls' is not? Or is it both?

Since the different expectations and perceptions that parents and teachers have of girls and boys strongly affect the messages, rewards, punishments, and models each child receives, the question of nature versus nurture becomes hard to answer. To further complicate the question, children obviously affect their parents as much as parents affect their children. If parents do, indeed, talk more to girl babies than to boy babies, are they *teaching* girls to be better listeners than boys, or are they *responding* to a sex difference? Let's see what research can tell us.

It's a Girl!

Socialization begins at birth. In fact, the sexual stereotypes believed by the parents of a female child *precede* her birth.

Consider the following statistics. H. Barry, M. Bacon, and I. L. Child, studying 110 cultures, found that 82 per cent of the people they polled expected females to be *more nurturing* than males; 87 per cent expected females to be *less achieving* than males; and 85 per cent expected females to be *less self-reliant* than males.

It seems that the way parents see their children is consisfent with what they expect to see. In one fascinating study, fathers were asked to rate their newborn children's characteristics, with the following results:

- Fathers of daughters rated their babies softer, finer featured, more awkward, less attentive, more delicate, and weaker than did fathers who rated sons.
- Fathers of sons found them to be firmer, larger featured, better co-ordinated, more alert, stronger, and harder than did fathers who rated daughters.

The most interesting aspect of this was that the birth lengths, weights, and reflex times for *all* babies in the study were the same!

From perceiving girls and boys differently according to stereotyped images, it is only a short step for parents to create *different realities* for each sex. Research has shown that

- Most girls are treated more protectively than boys. This logically suggests to girls that they must *need* protection.
- Most girls are complimented on their appearance before any other trait. People exclaim, 'What a pretty girl' but 'What a big, strong boy!' This, of course, conveys to girls that their packaging is very important.
- Most girls are handled with more vocalization than are boys. Michael Lewis found that mothers of twelve-week-old girls speak and respond more to the babbling of their babies than do mothers of sons.

The influence of socialization on female behaviour comes through loud and clear.

By eighteen months of age, girls already show more control over their tempers than do boys. But this sort of control can have a price.

Anxiety that is not directly related to a specific external cause often stems from fear of one's own unacceptable internal impulses. If girls are treated as though their aggressive, assertive, and achieving impulses are unexpected and even undesirable, we can logically anticipate a high anxiety level in young girls as they struggle to control these natural impulses.

Indeed, girls *do* experience much more anxiety than boys. Shocking confirmation of this can be found in a wide range of studies of different groups.

Fear of Failure vs. Need for Achievement

Fear of failure, like fear of success, is the legacy of nonassertiveness training. Fear of failure is the result of years of being shamed or teased by boys, brothers, fathers, mothers, or teachers whenever a public performance of athletic, mechanical, or combative prowess was attempted. Fear of success is the result of years of being warned against being 'too smart' or 'too strong' or 'too independent.' Where are the role models for strong, assertive women in our culture? Some can be found on the sports pages; there are a handful of world leaders to whom we can look; occasionally one hears about prominent business and professional women, or a barrier-smasher such as astronaut Sally Ride is thrust into public view. But these are the exceptions rather than the rule, and generally a major component of the message we get about them is how *unusual* they are.

Need for achievement, however, is built into all of us. It is an extension of our earliest desires to explore, crawl, walk, and run. It is a reflection of our ability to process information, formulate plans, and solve problems. It is an adult expression of our need to gain some control over our environment and solve some of its problems.

It's not uncommon for women to feel a mixture of fear of failure and need for achievement. The head-on collision between the two is what aggravates the female stress syndrome.

Fear of failure moves women away from their goals by involving them in excessive concern with the opinions of others. Failure then means shame, rather than just personal disappointment. Fear of failure requires constant collecting of excuses and a general defensiveness—both of which drain energy from directly pursuing goals! Women with a high fear of failure will constantly handicap themselves and increase their own stress in order to defend themselves against failure with excuses. For example, they may schedule too many things at the same time. Or they may never start a task until the last minute.

Sometimes women are not fully conscious of their ambivalence and the stress it imposes. Their nonassertiveness training has become so much a part of their way of being and their self-image that they don't even realize they are vacillating. At most, they may wonder why they feel so uncertain most of the time, or why they labour over making decisions.

Stress and The Singles Scene

Talk to a few single career women, and you will probably hear stories similar to Mickie's.

Mickie was single and successful. She was twenty-nine years old, however, and beginning to feel alone. Not lonely, she explained; *alone*. She wanted a partner. She wanted to meet a man who could join her and share in her life. Perhaps marry. Perhaps have children.

But Mickie was having a hard time. She found men she could 'adopt.' Men who would make great 'wives.' Men who would 'take her away from hard work and competition.' Men who would 'take care' of her. Men who truly believed she wanted to be 'dominated.' And men who truly believed that she wanted to 'mother' them. What she could not find was a man who believed her when she said she wanted a partner.

She was successful and loved her work. This made many men feel competitive. She was sexual and yet discriminating. This made many men feel anxious about 'performance.' She was mature and intelligent. This made many men feel self-conscious. She was self-supporting and financially secure. This made many men feel inadequate.

Mickie's story has a happy ending. She met a man who enjoyed her just as she had wanted to be enjoyed. Her independence was a bonus to him, not an escape from responsibility and not a threat. They are still living happily ever after, arguing about politics rather than about her achievements.

Not all such stories end so well, however. An achieving woman who harbours both fear of failure and fear of success tends to find herself devastated by male rejection, great or small. She blames herself for unsuccessful affairs. She retreats before her partner can. She 'obsesses' so much about past problems and future fantasies that, often, she cannot let things be. She may sabotage the relationships herself in order to explain possible failures or to avoid the responsibility of success.

In fact, the achieving single woman has only two options if she is interested in meeting men, neither of them very satisfactory. First, she can be socially nonassertive: that is, she can wait for men to telephone, ask her out to dinner, or initiate sexual advances. Or she can be socially assertive. That is, she can telephone men, invite them for dinner, and initiate sexual advances. The former option can make women feel powerless and stressed; the latter can make them feel vulnerable and stressed. Either way, they are single and stressed!

Retraining Yourself

As in other areas of the female stress syndrome, understanding the origins of a particular type of stress is only half the battle. Reducing that stress is the very important other half. If you feel that vacillating between the need for achievement and the fear of failure or fear of success is a long-term, chronic source of tension for you, try to bring the problem under control using these techniques.

1 Gather *information*, rather than opinions, about a problem or situation. This will increase your capacity to assess things realistically, and decrease the anticipatory anxiety you may be feeling.
2 Similarly, look at all situations involving your goals through *your* eyes only; don't try to see yourself as others see you. Looking at yourself to see if you appear to have failed will only hamper your ability to pursue goals.
3 Try to experience falling short of a goal as unfortunate, or as a learning experience, or as a disappointment, rather than as a failure.
4 Avoid self-blame at all times. Try your best, but don't put yourself on trial. Be your own defence lawyer—not the lawyer for the prosecution.
5 Be task-oriented rather than a praise addict. Focus on finishing a job, not showing it off, and you will reduce your performance anxiety and fear of failure at the same time.

FIVE

Love, Sex and Marriage Under Stress

Many psychologists and psychiatrists compare the state of being in love to that of temporary psychosis. The 'symptoms' are almost equally alarming.

- Reality becomes distorted, and a great deal of time is spent obsessively fantasizing about the future.
- Enormous power is bestowed on the loved one. His phone call can produce joy; his absence can produce anxiety; his approval becomes necessary for self-approval; his disapproval leads to self-blame. If he withdraws, we add self-insult to injury by assuming that he would not have done so if *we* had been more loving and understanding. We cannot proceed with our schedules, our plans, our daily lives until he has phoned, written, or made a date.
- Delusions of his perfection emerge and add to the flavour of insanity. Whatever his actual physical appearance, we imagine that he is the height of attractiveness, irresistible not only to ourselves but to others.

Instead of being alarmed, though, most of us seem to enjoy being in love, being in love makes us feel good. It lives up to all the clichés—we feel like we're walking on air, have stars in our eyes, and look younger than springtime. (Not a bad disorder, if you can get it!)

Nevertheless, it's also true that long-term relationships —and particularly marriages—create a special set of stresses for women. In fact, given the current high divorce rate, we might speculate that one major function of infatuation is to facilitate the otherwise terrifying process of marriage.

Unfortunately, many young women find themselves marrying in order to grow up. Even if she is still daughter, student, or in her late teens, a woman has 'adult' status once she is married. She is now a wife. She is Mrs Somebody. A new name, a new home, and a new adult life. But the teenage wife usually pays a high price for this instant new self-definition. She may bypass the identity confusion of these years, but she can become confused and overwhelmed by the responsibilities of marriage instead.

> At first Judy said no to Jack's proposal of marriage. She had wanted more in a husband—more maturity and more security. Jack was not quite tall enough, smart enough, or old enough to suit Judy's fantasies. Even his car was second-hand. But then she began to think about marriage in general rather than marriage to Jack. Married, she would not have to live at home nor ask permission to borrow the car. Married, she could give advice, not receive it. Married, she could dismiss forever the anxiety surrounding dateless weekends. Married, she could have a baby—dress it, take care of it, and show it off. Married, she would no longer feel her own life was second-hand. Judy said yes to Jack.
>
> Judy and Jack eloped. They set up home in a flat. Soon Jack quit university to work as a department-store salesman. Both Judy and Jack wanted more for him, but a baby was on the way, and they needed money. The baby and the baby blues arrived at the same time. Judy was constantly tired and lonely. She longed for the days of dates and romantic detours. She longed for her parents' home and the hot meals that she didn't have to prepare herself. What had she been thinking, she asked herself, when she had said yes to Jack?

Even if Judy had not eloped, stress would probably have developed after she had married. As both statistics and clinicians tell us, the act of marriage generally changes even the longest pre-marital live-in relationships. The factors that seem to be responsible can be labelled the 'four R's.'

1 *Regression*. Moving into a marriage may spark new plans for home life, but it also activates memories of our parents' marriage and home. With childhood memories come childhood feelings and behaviours. Husbands become confused with fathers and wives may act like daughters, much to their own horror.
2 *Re-creation*. Women may also find that despite their best intentions they are re-creating and perpetuating stereo-

typical, sexist behaviours. For example, they may find themselves displaying learned helplessness—imitating dependent behaviours that they observed to have worked for their mothers. They may find that they are suffering from the 'Cinderella complex'—waiting for the handsome prince to change their lives from emotional rags to riches. They may be acting out 'little woman' passivity—living in fear that they will be deserted if they become their own women. Or they may be slipping into nagging aggressiveness—sounding exactly like the women who most repelled them when they were young.

3 *Reaction.* To their surprise, some women find that they *react* more than they act. That is, they monitor their mate's moods and needs, trying to be perfect for him rather than being themselves. They watch every word to make sure that they are giving appropriate, justified responses. They hesitate to initiate plans, conversations, even sex, to avoid the responsibility that goes with self-assertion: plans may not work, conversations may become arguments, sexual overtures may be rejected. They soon feel like spectators of their own lives, and their sense of control erodes.

4 *Recollection.* Memories that may be confusing, unsettling, or stressful are often locked away through repression—a kind of motivated forgetting. This makes our daily lives easier. Marriage, however, can trigger the reappearance of recollections of our parents' marriage—of scenes, screams, and secrets. This, of course, makes coping more difficult. We may find that we are suffering from nightmares, unpleasant daydreams, mood swings, and a free-floating anxiety.

Fritz Perls, the originator of gestalt therapy, popularized the phrase 'here and now,' and warned us not to use the present to master the past. He observed that many of us re-create our most upsetting relationships of the past again and again to try to gain mastery of the past situation through the present re-enactment. Even if we should gain mastery in the present, however, it would not count because the *original* situation in the past would not have been settled—so we would be bound to set up the challenge once again. If you are having trouble moving out of the past and into the 'here and now,' try the following:

1 Look for evidence of the 'four R's' operating. Acknowledge to yourself which are causing you the most trouble.
2 Remind yourself that your increased awareness will permit you to make behavioural choices and take control of your interactions.
3 If you find it hard to believe that the present can be different from a replay of your past, just try behaving *as if* the present is different from the past. This will set up a positive, rather than negative, self-fulfilling prophecy! Both you and those around you will have a chance to try new actions and new reactions.

The 'four R's' are not the only sources of relationship stress. Females in this culture are often taught that they are the 'weaker sex,' but they may be rebelliously uncomfortable with emotional dependency. Since young women are often warned that men might want to use them as sex objects, they may be particularly wary of turning their sexual pleasure over to their partners. Since women often perceive that they may be traded in for a younger model in later years, they may be particularly focused on security. And since women in this culture are often warned that career is primary and marriage secondary for a man, they may deny feelings of rejection by fortifying themselves with anger and adopting a distant, 'I don't care' attitude.

Stress can also stem from a bad meshing of the expectations that a new couple usually brings together. Think of it this way: every relationship involves at least four sets of expectations—the woman's expectations for herself; the woman's expectations for her partner's behaviour; the man's expectations for himself; and the man's expectations for his partner's behaviour. There must be constant adjustment and communication of expectations in an ongoing relationship. And the stresses do not stop there.

• Add the problem of a woman who cannot meet her *own* learned self-expectations. She is likely to bring guilt, self-blame, and feelings of inadequacy to the relationship.

- Add the problem of multiple role conflicts, particularly prevalent in marriage. That is, a woman often finds that her roles as mother, daughter, and friend conflict with the behaviours expected of a wife.
- Add the problems created as role models keep rapidly changing, as they have in the 1970s and 1980s. Doris Day has given way to Mary Tyler Moore, and she, in turn, to Sally Ride!
- Add the problems of women who preferred their fathers to their mothers as role models in many areas. Such women are usually well-adjusted, high achievers, but they are unlikely to fit into a conventional role.
- Add the special problems of those women who did not have adequate or acceptable female role models at all.

Unfortunately, there is no second chance at childhood. To make relationships work without excessive stress, we must parent ourselves in those areas where our parents were inadequate. We cannot expect our partners to make up for the past.

Go even one step further to take control over *your* daily life by giving yourself permission to develop your own set of relationship expectations. When you do, be realistic; know both yourself and your mate. We are all package deals! Take the bad with the good, the weaknesses with the strengths—develop roles that take both sides into account. Remember, your relationship is made up of you and him—nobody else. It is shaped by who the two of you are, not who you *should* be.

Manipulation Tactics

Loving relationships involve a degree of 'letting go,' accepting vulnerability, and sharing control—admitting that you care about and can be affected by your mate's behaviour. But if couples struggle against dreaded feelings of vulnerability and struggle for a sense of control, they will create fights to serve both functions. Through fights they try to convince themselves that they 'don't care,' that they can upset their partner, that they can hurt more than be hurt. Through fights they avoid close, intimate moments and warm, caring feelings, which might be so desperately needed that the thought of losing such a bond becomes worse than pretending the bond doesn't exist in the first place.

If the real point of a fight turns out to be reducing the stress of vulnerability and/or loss of control, rather than solving the issue at hand, one or more of the following manipulation tactics will appear. Check yourself on this inventory.

MANIPULATION

TACTIC	DEFINITION	YES	NO
Mind-reading	Telling your mate what he thinks or feels, despite his protests to the contrary.		
Sleuthing	Collecting clues and evidence consistent with your own fears and dire prophecies.		
Grab-bagging	Reaching into the past to grab at insults and injustices you have saved up for fights or flights.		
Name-calling	Teasing and taunting your mate in a way which ensures that anxiety-provoking issues will not get faced squarely.		
Running scared	Behaving in ways you think will protect you from disappointments		

	that have not yet happened (and may never happen).
Replaying	Re-running and reviewing upsetting or frightening memories again and again to keep yourself on guard against being vulnerable to your mate.

Fights that rely on manipulation tactics are a sign of stress. But, as with all stress, trying to deal with the *symptoms* alone has at best only short-term benefits. Dealing with the underlying dynamics of the relationship will have long-term consequences, since these dynamics can either aggravate or ease relationship stress. Let's look at some of them.

Dynamics That Aggravate Relationship Stress

Projection

A man who flies into a rage if his partner procrastinates on a commitment may be fighting his own embarrassing tendency to procrastinate at the office. A woman who panics or sulks at the least sign of her mate flirting may secretly feel that she herself could take a flirtation too far. In such ways, partners may 'project' their own unacceptable thoughts, feelings, and impulses onto the other.

This style of handling incidents on a daily basis can greatly increase the stress level of the relationship. Take the case of Jim.

Jim had had a bad day at the office, an annoying drive home on the crowded motorway, and an upsetting conversation with his accountant. When he finally reached home his regular parking space was occupied. Jim would feel much better if he could let off some steam, if he could find someone to blame for his day, if he could yell a bit. Jim knows, however, that this 'fight' impulse is 'unacceptable.' In reality, there is no one to blame for his unfortunate day. He would, in fact, feel very guilty if he took out his frustrations on his wife and equally innocent children.

Solution? Perceive his *wife* as starting a fight! He searches for a look on her face that might suggest dissatisfaction or demand, and, of course, he finds it. Jim gets to have his fight and lets off steam without feeling guilty or consciously responsible. The price, however, is steep.

Displacement

By definition, displacement involves reducing potential guilt by redirecting a feeling from its original source toward a safer person or object. Have you ever kicked your cat after talking to your mother? Slammed the door while your baby was crying? That's displacement.

Taken further, displacement can put stress on relationships. 'You always hurt the one you love' can be more accurately stated as, 'You only dare to hurt the one who loves you.' A man who appears mild-mannered to the outside world may be touchy and quick-tempered with his mate. A woman who rages at her partner when he asks her to do something she considers excessive may not be able to raise her voice to her boss when he makes unreasonable demands.

Dependency

Although dependency can be healthy and a strong bond between two people, it can also be destructive and undermining. Confusing a mate with a mother or father encourages childlike reactions and muddles the present with past memories. Remember, to avoid falling into a dependent relationship that leaves one partner a child, both people must understand that there are no second chances at childhood. Caring is, of course, different from care-taking. The former is a form of loving; the latter is manipulative and can be destructive.

Aggression

The important distinction between aggression and assertion is its intent. During assertion, we move ourselves *toward* another; during aggression, we move ourselves *against* another. Assertion is vital within a relationship. Aggression is not.

It's difficult for women to be assertive when they have been raised with the notion that they should spend their days doing office or house work, but act like the weaker sex. Many of us fear displeasing others, fear abandonment, fear appearing too independent. The truth is, reports indicate that both men and women enjoy a partner who is assertive. Such a partner eliminates the need for mind-reading. Such a partner gives his or her mate implicit permission to be similarly assertive. Aggression, however, often evokes more aggression.

Passivity
Passivity and evasion are very manipulative and are used to seize power within the relationship without assuming the responsibility for it.

Passivity can be an aggressive act. A familiar example is the man or woman who, with an outward show of co-operation, does not accompany his or her mate to a party. ('You go ahead, dear, I'll be perfectly fine here at home'), or who goes but sits passive and uninvolved. Either way, the couple is deprived of having a good time *together*.

Sexual Withdrawal
Sexual withdrawal can be powerfully manipulative. Through sexual withdrawal a partner can be saying 'I will not give to you, nor will I put my pleasure in your hands. I no longer feel comfortable letting you know that you can have an effect on me.'

There are many problems with this dynamic. First, it sets up a pattern of bringing nonsexual problems into the bedroom. Second, it is indirect and does not effectively address the real cause of the anger. Third, it deprives *both* members of the couple, not just the partner being punished!

Sex and Female Stress

Women seem to have been raised amid conflicting sexual messages. They face at least four different sexual dilemmas.

1 *The fear of saying 'yes' versus the fear of saying 'no.'* To say 'yes'
   involves taking responsibility for birth control, moni-
   toring male methods of contraception, or risking an
   unwanted pregnancy. To say 'no' involves risks rangeing
   from rape to angry rejection.

2 *Performance anxiety versus castration concerns.* If a woman
   absorbs advice on 'How to Please Your Man,' she may
   become a spectator during her own sexual encounters
   and suffer from performance anxiety severe enough to
   inhibit her own sexual response. If, on the other hand,
   she absorbs advice on 'How to Maximize Your Sexual
   Pleasure,' she runs the risk of frightening off men who
   may see requests as instructions, advances as aggression, interest as promiscuity, playfulness as manipulation, and passion as competition.

3 *Fear of discovery versus fear of frustration.* Women all seem to
   be potentially embarrassed by their sexuality. There is
   someone, in almost every case, from whom they would
   prefer to hide their sexuality. More frequently than
   not, even husbands are unaware of their wives' capacity
   to masturbate or fantasize. Frustration, however, is an
   unsatisfactory alternative. To deny or hide these needs
   may not only add to the female stress syndrome, but
   deprive women of a natural stress antidote—satisfying
   sex.

4 *Dyadic duet versus do-your-own-thing.* Humans seem to be a
   bonding species, and women, particularly, find themselves looking for long-term partners. Too much emphasis on finding a husband and defining oneself in
   terms of *his* success, however, has led to a reaction
   among women against the 'Cinderella complex.' Too
   much emphasis on going it alone seems to be equally
   unsatisfying, however. Betty Friedan suggests in her
   book *The Second Stage* that the trick will be to find new
   ways of working *with* men to build and rebuild lives,
   rather than bailing out of bonding altogether. Finding a
   balance, then, is an ongoing problem contributing to
   female stress and low sexual desire.

Sometimes female sexuality becomes a victim of motherhood's stresses: less time, less privacy, more distractions,

fear of another pregnancy, self-consciousness about body changes and concerns about adequacy as a mother.

To make matters worse, a mother's own sexual desire can become a victim too. She may feel that she no longer *should* be either sexy to her husband, or sexual in her own interests. Too often, her husband may feel the same way. He would feel guilty if he allowed himself to have sexual feelings about a 'mother,' so he experiences a mysterious loss of desire or arousal instead—the Madonna Complex.

As sex fades from a couple's life, stress grows. An important expression of adult affection has been lost. An important source of physical pleasure has been lost. An important type of stimulation and punctuation of a routinized life has been lost. An important aspect of love has been lost. Such a couple must rediscover each other as *people*, remind themselves that they are entitled to sexual pleasure—entitled to each other!

Relationship-Stress Management

Here are some ideas for managing the stresses inherent in relationships.

1 Remind your mate and yourself that you are a team—both on the same side.
2 Communicate to be heard, not to win.
3 Realize that it is not your job to teach your mate right and wrong.
4 Don't confuse compliance with caring, nor lack of compliance with lack of caring.
5 Principles are rarely more important than people. Find room for both!
6 Make requests, not demands. Requests are flattering and usually fulfilled. Demands are challenging, and often resisted.
7 *Ask* for what you need. Don't wait for your partner to develop mental telepathy! In the meantime, work on communication and speaking your mind. This will give your mate implicit permission to do the same, and no one will be forced to play twenty questions.
8 Develop imaginary role-reversal skills. They add

empathy and sympathy to relationships. Put yourself in his place and help him understand how you see things. You will be less likely to take his behaviour personally if you do.

9 Acknowledge that perfect fits do not exist; go for compromise and points for effort.

10 Recognize jealousy; it is a common human reaction. Can a father be jealous of his own children? Can a mother be jealous of her own husband? Of course. Don't deny these feelings or they will operate autonomously—treat them as real and you can give them perspective and limits.

11 View yourself through your own eyes. Give yourself permission to relax, speak for yourself, and be good to yourself. Know yourself as you *are*, not as you think you should be.

12 Try to be your own parent. It's a chance to raise yourself the way you would have wanted to be raised. Don't look to your mate to compensate for your parents' inadequacies; and don't try to parent him.

13 Permit yourself the vulnerability that comes with normal bonding. Know that you can put yourself in your partner's hands, both literally and figuratively. We bond to produce friendships. We bond to produce families. We bond to produce love.

Sometimes, no matter how much effort you put into trying to understand the dynamics of a relationship, you will not be able to alter behaviours and expectations that are firmly entrenched or operating on automatic pilot. If the problem seems to be unyielding, remember that you can always turn to professional counselling, either for yourself alone or for the two of you as a couple. A marriage counsellor, may be just what you need to help you pinpoint the sources of stress and heal a troubled relationship.

SIX

Mothering and the Female Stress Syndrome

Imagine this: A fourteen-hour work day. A seven-day work week. No minimum wage, no pension plan, no expense account, no promotion, no lunch hour, no drinks after work, and no paid holiday guaranteed. Men need not apply.

Sound familiar? Despite its appalling job description, every year many thousands of women sign up for motherhood. It is the fringe benefits they are after: participation in creation, touching life and lives, loving, sharing, and caring. For these pay-offs they think they are willing to pay the price. Too often, however, the price is steeper in stress than they bargained for.

Mothering Today

The female stress syndrome is probably as old as motherhood itself. What is new is the size of the problem. Rates of both depression and anxiety reactions have been climbing since the 1940s. Furthermore, record numbers of women are choosing to postpone motherhood, forgo motherhood, or pursue a full-time career during motherhood, an option that carries its own brand of stress. Why?

Sagging Support System

Although kitchen technology has freed the housewife from hours of physical labour, progress has created problems too. Harriet's experiences are common.

Harriet left the small town where she had grown up to attend university. Through her new roommate, she was introduced to Alex. They dated for two years and then married. Alex became an account executive for a national corporation and was asked to relocate. Within thirty-two months of leaving her home. Harriet had moved, married, moved again, and suspended her education, and was now pregnant. She did part-time work

54

during her pregnancy in order to save a little extra money for baby costs and found little time to meet her new neighbours or continue her education. By the time the baby arrived, Harriet was feeling alone and stressed.

Separated from her family and hometown, Harriet was separated from an important mothering support system. Years ago a new mother was helped by her own mother and even her grandmother. Now, however, families are usually split into units small enough to move to locations that offer jobs.

Instead of turning to her mother and grandmother for advice, today's mobile young housewife must turn to the 'experts.' Unfortunately, when she does, she gets too much information. 'How to' books are everywhere. Child experts speak from car radios, television sets, and cassette tapes and write newspaper columns and magazine features.

The mass media have replaced grandmother! But whereas grandmother's advice was consistent, today's myriad experts offer myriad opinions. The young mother is soon completely confused.

The Working Mother

Working may help women relieve the family budget squeeze, but it also contributes to stress. Women do not trade in housework for job work; they *add* job duties to home and mothering duties.

Working mothers often worry that they may be cheating their families of their time, and so they try to make it up to them. This in turn leaves the working mother even more tired, still guilt-ridden, and without any time for herself.

Often working mothers must deal also with sexism—and not just sexism at their place of employment, either. Many women report that as working mothers they are discriminated against by their children's teachers, school committee members, and neighbours, and within their own families by critical parents, in-laws, or even husbands.

Betty and Joe had four children. They both agreed that the children needed Betty at home full time, but as Joe's salary increments fell behind cost-of-living increases, Betty had to take a nine-to-five job. Soon after starting work, Betty was called to school by the teacher of her eldest son. The teacher reported that the boy seemed to be having difficulty concentrating on his classwork. She suggested that Betty's new job and schedule might be upsetting her son and interfering with his ability to concentrate.

Feeling upset and guilty, Betty called the boy's grandparents and received two versions of what she calls the 'Mother's Place Is in the Home' lecture. Her husband suggested that they increase discipline and not indulge the boy. Betty's best friend disagreed and suggested family counselling.

Things did not improve until a state-wide intelligence test given in school showed that Betty's son was extremely gifted and probably very bored in the classroom. His classroom problems coincided with his mother's new job, but were not caused by her working. He was skipped a class, Betty kept her job, and all was well. Or was it? Betty learned how quickly her working could be held responsible for her family's problems. She also learned how ready she was to do the same.

The alternative seems to create stress as well. That is, a mother who chooses to stay home runs the risk of feeling that she is not doing her share to relieve her husband of the economic strain of these times. Furthermore, her sense of dependency is heightened even as she clips coupons and pinches pennies. It seems that mothers in the 1980s are likely to feel stressed and guilty if they do work outside the house, and stressed and guilty if they do not.

Divorced, single, and widowed mothers, of course, usually have very little choice about whether they work. It is obvious that money stress is considerable in single-parent households.

A different kind of stress is created for modern mothers by what I'll call 'Dana's Dilemma.' Dana is a friend who confided recently, 'I'd be much happier at home than I am working.' Since financial considerations were not the motivation for Dana's job, I asked why she did not remain at home. 'I feel that being a wife and a mother is my thing, but I don't have any friends to do my thing *with* anymore,' she replied.

It seems that most of Dana's friends left the PTA in order to return to college or pursue careers. In fact, they scolded Dana for not doing the same. Social pressure on women to 'do their own thing,' Dana claims, apparently does not encompass staying home and mothering.

'A Mother's Work Is Never Done . . .'

Current popular social pressures on women to reject the conventional sex-roles often mean that mothers and housewives feel the stress of low status. Since women need no experience, no entrance exam, no pre-requisites, no courses, and no degrees to become mothers, the role is frequently thought to be low in prestige and exclusiveness —and not just by men (see 'Dana's Dilemma,' page 56). Furthermore, the average housewife spends between fifty and seventy-five hours a week on housecleaning and other physical labour: bending, pulling, pushing, zipping, wiping, catching, patching, lifting, lugging, and hugging. Since when has physical labour added to the attractiveness of a social position?

It is true that women no longer have to bake their own bread or churn ice cream for the kiddies, but just look at the list of chores that still must be done.

bathing children
cooking
disciplining
dishwashing
dusting
feeding family
feeding pets
laundering
managing finances
organizing children's
  play
picking up after the
  family
repairing or arranging
  repairs
scrubbing floors,
  windows, etc.
shopping, menu
  planning
vacuuming

Beyond Housework

Beyond household duties are the stresses that include loss of freedom, some isolation, and much monotony. Not that these problems are exclusive to the mother—the secretary, executive, and cab driver may have the same complaints. An important difference, though, is that the secretary, executive, and cab driver have other adults around; the full-time mother usually does not. She waits all day for her husband, who may be too tired to talk when he returns home from work.

The list of stresses associated with mothering goes on and on.

Mother's Stress Checklist

Nine-to-five hours? Call in for a sick day? Maternity leave from maternity? Not a chance! High risk for the female stress syndrome? Without a doubt!

If you are a mother, fill out this mother's stress checklist and see how high a risk you're running. To the left of each item, write your points according to the following scale:

0   NEVER TRUE
1   RARELY TRUE
2   SOMETIMES TRUE
3   FREQUENTLY TRUE
4   ALWAYS TRUE

ACTIVITIES

I can completely lose interest in social activities and hobbies; the effort seems too great. ☐

I find it difficult to know what I would like to do with free time. ☐

I forget what chore I have started and don't follow through with plans. ☐

I start more projects than I can possibly finish. ☐

I feel the house must be spotless and run with complete efficiency. ☐

I find myself feeling overwhelmed and out of control because there are too many demands on me. ☐

I find it hard to say no to my children or husband, even when I think I am right to say no. ☐

SELF-CONCEPT

I feel that my appearance doesn't really matter to me or anyone else. ☐

I feel that there is very little time for me in my day. ☐

I think other people's opinions are more valid than mine. ☐

I feel unappreciated by my family. ☐
I fantasize about what my life would be like if I could start again. ☐
I find I exaggerate and boast to friends. ☐
I feel a sense of resentment and anger that I cannot really explain. ☐
I find that I often look for compliments and praise. ☐

APPETITE

I feel too aggravated or tense to eat. ☐
I crave coffee or cigarettes to keep me going. ☐
I binge and then regret it. ☐
I need chocolate and/or other carbohydrates when I feel tired or down. ☐
I suffer from nausea, cramps, or diarrhoea. ☐
I snack too often. ☐

SLEEP

I have trouble falling asleep. ☐
I awaken earlier than I need/want to. ☐
I have nightmares. ☐
I do not feel rested even when I have a full night's sleep. ☐
I fall asleep earlier than I want to in the evening. ☐
I seem to need a nap in the afternoon. ☐
I awaken during the night. ☐

OUTLOOK

I feel like I've lost my sense of humour. ☐
I feel impatient and irritable. ☐
I cry without knowing why. ☐
I relive the past. ☐
I am pessimistic about the future. ☐
I feel numb and emotionless. ☐
I find myself laughing nervously, too loudly, or without reason. ☐
I ignore things that would upset me. ☐
I am sorry that I chose motherhood. ☐

TOTAL

If your score is between *1 and 40*, congratulations! You are at *low risk* for the female stress syndrome, since you seem to have a sense of control and are managing your maternal career well.

If your score is between *41 and 75*, you are probably *mildly stressed* by mothering and may experience some transient stress symptoms.

If your score is between *76 and 110*, you are running a *moderate risk* for the female stress syndrome. Use the self-help advice in this book to lower your stress levels.

If your score is between *111 and 148*, you are in the *high stress* range, and this book is particularly important for you!

Managing Motherhood

What to do when a mother is burned-out blue? What to do when she feels taken for granted, tired, unappreciated, and unattractive? What to do if that mother is you?

Begin by re-examining your role honestly. List the advantages of motherhood for *you*. Perhaps it is nurturing, perhaps feeling needed, perhaps being in control, perhaps being an authority figure, perhaps shaping decisions, perhaps being in the centre of a family, or perhaps enjoying children's activities yourself. As your sense of choice about motherhood increases, stress stimulated by resentment will decrease.

Then re-examine your expectations for yourself as a mother. Are you realistic? How closely do your priorities match your routines? Which of these elements needs adjusting? (Often this is not an easy question to answer, so give it a lot of thought.)

In addition, every mother must become her own sympathetic permission-giver. Do you usually feel that you must be overworked and overtired before you let yourself rest? Do you feel that you have to justify time off to your husband, your mother-in-law, and the rest of the world? Was your hospital stay after the birth of your last child your last morning in bed? *Why?*

Mothers who wait to be rescued by others become disappointed, angry, and stressed: disappointed because any rescue that does come will probably not be well timed;

angry because they have given a great deal of power to others; stressed because they must continually show the world that they need rescuing. Mothers who feel entitled to rest, relaxation, and realistic expectations can give themselves the permission they need to avoid the female stress syndrome. They can be good to themselves. They can appreciate attention and considerations from others as important extras, rather than as too little, too late.

SEVEN

Stress and the Working Woman

The New Woman

It is estimated at the beginning of this decade that approximately 90 per cent of the female population has worked or will work for pay at some time in their lives. A number of interesting factors combine to make the percentage so high.

Birth Control
For the first time in history, women control the timing of their children. The time before, in between, and after childbirth and child raising can be planned to a greater extent than ever before.

Kitchen Technology
Modern materials and machines save time, energy, and physical wear and tear. Convenience foods reduce cooking time—or even eliminate it altogether.

Re-examination of Anatomical Destiny
It has occurred to many people that if a woman can work and bring home a salary, a man can manage a household and raise children. Most jobs today are service jobs that require brains rather than brawn. Even in physical work, such as firefighting or military combat training, women are proving their ability to hold their own. By choice or by necessity, both sexes are broadening their views about what different people can do for a living.

Inflation and Recession
Two incomes are not only better than one—they will probably be necessary to maintain a decent standard of living in the future and to carry a family over a period of strikes or unemployment.

Divorce

The divorce rate continues to climb. No more can women count on 'lifetime employment' as housewives or home-makers; nor, on the other hand, can they count on alimony. Alimony is going out of style—legally, practically, and socially. Divorced women work to support themselves, their children, and, often, their independence. Working provides the financial base for life choices that are alternatives to remarriage.

'Dutch Treat' Marriages

Women are staying single longer now than ever before. Their finances develop with their careers, and they see themselves as self-supporting individuals. The women's movement, of course, has reinforced the idea of personal autonomy in the economic as well as the emotional sphere—for both sexes. Thus, when one of these women ties the knot, the result is often what I call a 'dutch treat' marriage. Both husband and wife maintain their own finances as when they were single, or they share expenses according to convenience or individual income.

Nine-to-Five Plus

Although women have re-entered the job market, research backs up women's own observations that they are still expected to execute their traditional roles at home as well as their duties at work.

Working women carry out dual roles in response to their own expectations, as well as their husbands' expectations. We have learned our roles through custom and culture, and we are no less hard on ourselves than are those around us. We run from board meetings to PTA meetings, monitor supermarket receipts, deal with demanding supervisors and recalcitrant repair people. We are stressed and resentful, driven and guilt-ridden, and we are convinced that that's the way things are supposed to be.

Dual Roles, Dual Stresses

Working women with dual roles are stressed in ways not

usually shared by working men, or by nonworking women.

Although being a full-time housewife has its own stresses, in some ways it is the easier side of the coin. Compare the role of wife or parent to that of a working woman. As a wife or parent

- No exams, prerequisites, or previous experience are necessary.
- There is no need to submit a resumé for the job.
- Failures are usually not observed, analysed, and judged in public. They can be hidden in the privacy of the home.
- There is no competition on the job. The laundry is all yours!
- There is no competition *for* the job. Your children are all yours!
- There is no time clock. Your schedule is yours to structure—no doubt it's filled beyond the waking hours, but it is still all yours.
- You are your own supervisor and boss. This is not to say that you are not your severest critic and slave-driver. On the contrary, at home you probably assume more responsibility than if you did have a boss. It is a different kind of stress trade-off, however, than that involved in working for a boss.

Working women who are wives and/or mothers often live with a sharp conflict between their roles inside and outside the home. Many mothers who work part time report that they cannot feel satisfied in either role. When they are working, they can think only of the child at home. When they are home, they feel they should be on the job.

Women who work full time, on the other hand, may feel guilty that they were away from home all day. When they come home, they begin to compensate rather than relax. They put in extra effort and activity at home as if they had been playing all day.

Of course, arriving home after a hard day at the office, women can feel resentful of children's and husbands' demands—and then feel distressed by their own resentment. Too often this leads to an ongoing marital debate about whose job or income is more important to the family's survival. Since the husband's income is usually designated for the utilities and other running costs, and the wife's income more often provides the 'extras,' husbands seem to have the upper hand. If the discrepancy in income is sizable, the debate may have some minor merit. If there is little discrepancy in income, however, the two salaries might just as well be considered part of a pool of financial resources. The 'extras' that a wife's income provides, usually turn out to be such non-frivolous items as the family car, the family trip, and even the family's food. Jenny's case is not uncommon.

> Jenny's husband took paternalistic pride in her early successes as a dress designer. He helped her make contacts and develop bookkeeping skills. As her business grew, he was less needed and she was less available. She had her own stories to tell and her own business trips to take. He demanded that she choose between her business and him. She offered him the same choice to point out the absurdity of his request. He, of course, said he could never give up his business and that his involvement in it did not mean that he did not love her. She said the same was true for her. 'It's different for a woman,' he replied. 'I'm sorry to hear that you feel that way,' she said. She also said goodbye.

Not all women would, could, or should say goodbye in a situation like Jenny's. Not all women would find themselves in such a situation. Too many, however, do. Too many must then struggle with realistic alternatives. My most heartfelt professional advice to such women is this: if you are thinking of leaving your marriage because you would prefer to live *alone* than to live with the stress of the relationship, a separation may work for you. If, however, you are leaving your marriage for a fantasy of another, more perfect husband—reconsider. People are package deals, and we cannot order the options to suit us at will. Job and marriage co-ordination creates problems for all of us; don't jump to blame the stress on your spouse.

Not Just One of the Boys

Whether a woman is married or not, childless or not, the

nature of the on-the-job stress is part of what separates the 'girls' from the 'men.' The sources of this stress are many, but the most prevalent are the fear of success and the problem of sexism.

The handicapping effect of the fear of success has been widely analysed. *It is real.* Given society's emphasis on appearance and passivity in females, working women may fear that career or job success will make them less attractive. Unfortunately, research bears them out. Even more unfortunately, this stereotyping is practised by women as well as men.

The origins of women's fear of success, then, are not mysterious. Many were discussed in Chapter 4. Others are personal to each individual. Sexism, however, is universal.

Sexism comes in many forms, some subtle, some overt.

- Demeaning comments depicting women as sex objects.
- Vulgar jokes meant to embarrass women and place them in a position of being a spoilsport if they object.
- Condescension by men, whatever their relative position or rank in the office.
- Misuse of 'occupational power' by men who will make sexual innuendoes and advances toward women who lack job security or union protection.
- Job discrimination, precipitating two types of stress: the stress of gathering evidence and seeking legal redress, and the stress of deciding whether or not to pursue that course.

There is a direct link between sexism and female stress. As our sense of control is lowered, our sense of stress is increased, and the very focus of sexism is the lowering of women's control over their own lives. We feel that we have little power to influence our occupational destiny. Exposure to sexism fosters stress, and fighting sexism increases it.

The Type A Woman

Given the special stresses that working, career, and professional women are subject to, it is no wonder that they experience female stress symptoms. Given the special drive and character women must have to compete successfully and even to excel in the working world, it is no wonder that they suffer 'executive stress' symptoms as well.

According to researchers, Meyer Friedman and Ray Rosenman, achievement-oriented male executives have long paid for their personality profile with high blood pressure and/or heart disease. The same characteristics that were reinforced by their career successes were making them susceptible to psychosomatic diseases. These characteristics include

aggressiveness
competitiveness
focus on approval of
  others for their self-
  esteem

impatience and
  irritability
perfectionism
secret anger

Friedman and Rosenman labelled this profile the Type A personality.

Now, as women are entering executive careers, they are exhibiting their own brand of Type A behaviour. Imagine the Type A personality as a working woman, and the result is the following:

- She is a perfectionist, and so must be the perfect employee without slacking off as beauty, devoted daughter, lover, wife, mother, friend.
- She is never satisfied with her achievements.
- She is as impatient and irritable as the Type A man, but unfortunately has less time and more chores to be impatient and irritable about!
- She can be aggressive rather than assertive.
- She gives others enormous power to affect her feelings about herself through their reactions to her.
- She is secretly angry that no man is saving her from herself, although she would like to feel differently.

When a man exhibits Type A behaviour, doctors and family become concerned. 'Get a thorough checkup,' they say. 'Take a holiday.' However, this advice is not as readily applied to Type A women, most of whom have family and social responsibilities they can't easily escape—or which they *feel* they can't easily escape, which amounts to the same thing. Too often, they simply find themselves settling for the notion that everything will look a lot better after a good night's sleep.

A good night's sleep can't hurt, but it will not be enough to reduce the stress symptoms of a Type A woman. Better advice? First of all, educate yourself about stress in general; about your particular stress pattern; about the opportunities for stress management in your daily life. Take *control* of your life. Don't give others the power to affect your self-esteem and behaviour with their approval or disapproval. Decide for yourself how you feel about yourself. Don't give others the power to control your time schedule unless it is appropriate. Don't give others the power to control your goals through implicit or explicit competition. You must concentrate on winning your own self-approval, scheduling your time yourself, and setting and achieving your own goals.

On the very practical side, here are some suggestions from other working women.

1 Buy more clothes and underwear to avoid the need for frequent laundry and cleaning trips. You save time for every penny you spend.
2 Hire help, as much as you can afford. Find a cleaning service. Let the tailor fix your hems, the laundry do your washing. Use caterers for parties. Teenagers and students are good sources for many services. Don't overlook a tax accountant.
3 Schedule escape. Read a novel in the bath, on the bus, or at lunchtime. If your body can't go to a faraway island, at least your psyche can.
4 Find private time. One half hour after everyone else has gone to sleep or before everyone else has awakened can be *your* time.
5 Play. If you enjoy games, take a crossword puzzle to breakfast, or backgammon to dinner.
6 If you have a mate who works, establish a policy of 'equal flexibility.' Each of you must be able to take it for granted that your goal is to share the household work equally. Whoever had the easier day or who got home first would

prepare the dinner. If neither of you has time or energy, you might go out, order in, or even eat separately.

7 Determine the healthiest diet for you and make sure you have the right foods on hand.

8 Keep lists. Whether in the form of a small notebook or pocket calendar that is always in your purse. Such a system will enable you to trap thoughts, names, addresses, dates, and so on as they come to you and to get things done efficiently. Again, taking control of your environment lowers stress.

9 Self-hypnosis and other special relaxation exercises can be a great help in relieving tension. See Chapter 10.

The Benefits of Working

Hard as it may be to believe, despite all the stresses associated with working, its benefits are enormous. An important antidote to the female stress syndrome is the kind of support system most work environments offer— the network of co-workers.

• Working can provide social contacts and a sense of belonging. Spending almost half your waking life during the week with any group of people is bound to facilitate ties. Sometimes lifelong friends are made at work. Sometimes the friendships are unique to the work place. Either way, the relationships can be valuable and supportive. Either way, you are part of a team. A fundamental need for belonging is to some degree filled.

• Working can provide different points of view. Talking about problems with your work network can broaden your perspective on any topic. It can help you understand another's behaviour in a less personalized way. It can help you re-interpret last night's domestic fight or this morning's news bulletin. It can bring you into conversation with men and women from other backgrounds, generations, and businesses.

• Working can provide humour. Heard any good jokes lately? If so, and if you work, you probably heard them at the office.

• Working can provide resources. Your workmates may

have ideas, information, and know-how that you do not, and vice versa.

- Working can provide confidants. Who understands your work frustrations and elations better than someone who is also doing the same work? Who would be safer to talk to about family problems than someone who is *not* in the family?

- Working can provide cushioning and escape valves for anger. You can tear into your work, instead of into your mother-in-law. You can beat a dead-line instead of a dead issue. You can argue for a proposal, instead of arguing against your husband.

- Working can provide sympathy. The communal expressions of sympathy for sorrow that you get from the office are a unique source of support. Your workmates are a semipublic group, wider than your family yet not as impersonal as strangers or polite neighbours. The larger the group, furthermore, the more likely that you will find others who have experienced the same sorrow.

- Working can provide adult conversation and intellectual stimulation. Many women take part-time jobs or volunteer their work just to spend at least part of their day with other adults.

- Working can provide a source of praise and reassurance. Too often, good or extra work at home is taken for granted or goes unnoticed altogether. Although this is possible on the job too, more often you will be told if your work is good. Promotions and salaries are tangible proof of performance.

- Working can provide objective feedback. Your own family, appreciative or otherwise, can't really be considered objective. In the work place, you and your work are evaluated often, by many people who have no interest in you other than how effectively you are doing your job. You can base further actions and decisions on impartial data, which increases your sense of identity and control. A great stress reliever!

EIGHT

Hidden Stresses

They are all around, distracting you, wearing away at your patience, creating anxious anticipation. They produce fatigue, irritability, and tension. They are subtle, however; they sometimes hit and run. They are the hidden stresses contributing to the Female Stress Syndrome.

Hidden Stress: Driving

Mary glanced at the clock and realized that she had not left enough time for the ride to her daughter's nursery school. She grabbed her coat and bag, ran to the car, and pulled out of her driveway into traffic. She noticed that she did not have time to fill up the petrol tank. For the rest of the trip, one eye was on the tank indicator, and one ear was listening for a sputtering engine.

Her thoughts were on the inconvenience to her daughter's teacher created by her lateness, and she increased her speed. Within a half minute, Mary heard a siren behind her. Her heart seemed to jump as she searched the rear view mirror for a police car. Instead she saw an ambulance, and pulled over to the side of the road to permit its passage. Now she was even more late. Again Mary merged into traffic and picked up speed. Just as she did so, the car on her left crossed into her lane without signalling. Mary swerved automatically and came close to creating her own accident. She was now stuck behind this car and forced to inch along or to pass on the left illegally.

She passed, picked up speed again, and rushed to a red light. The light seemed to be the longest she had ever encountered, and she decided it was broken. She was about to risk going through the red light when it changed to green. She started up again, only to be stopped three more times by long red lights.

She wanted to scream, or to cry. Either would have felt better than sitting in her car like a prisoner while her daughter and her teacher waited endlessly in the schoolyard.

Does Mary's adventure sound familiar? Short-distance driving is a major source of stress, and suburban women must deal with this stress daily. Much of their day is spent chauffeuring: to the dentist; to get the children haircuts; to the railway station and back again; to town; to the supermarket; to the school; to the post office or the cleaners.

Since stress increases as control and predictability decrease, driving is one of the most stressful of daily activities. It demands high levels of visual-motor skills, good judgment, vigilance, experience, caution, technical knowledge, and a defensive mentality. The consequences associated with mistakes in this activity range from costly repair to encounters with the law to bodily harm and death.

Hidden Stress: Waiting

In a survey of more than four hundred women, 'waiting' was consistently listed as a not-so-hidden pet peeve. Most women, feel that many of their most frustrating minutes are spent waiting for people: their mates or their dates, their children, repairers and preparers. If they are mothers they wait for babysitters and doctors. If they are working women they wait in bank queues, lift queues, and commuter queues. Even the ladies' room at a theatre has a longer queue than that for the men's room. Low control? Yes. High stress? Absolutely.

Hidden Stress: Entertaining

Another source of female burnout is entertaining. This is typically 'women's work,' and it is filled with labour: shopping, cleaning, dicing, cooking, serving, setting, and cleaning (again).

The stresses associated with entertaining vary, of course, from time to time, and from woman to woman, but a number of generalizations can be made.

1 Preparing your own food involves the risk of outcomes ranging from 'nothing special' to 'disaster.'

2 Co-ordinating the timing of many dishes and many guests can tax your sense of control.

3 Entertaining on short notice adds time pressures and interferes with the planning process.

4 Entertaining strangers raises additional problems. It is difficult to predict their food preferences, their humour, and their interests. If the strangers are business associates, it is difficult to predict the importance of the visit. If the strangers are new family members or new acquaintances, you may feel that you are being judged.

5 Entertaining in-laws: performance stress.

6 Entertaining friends: competition stress.

7 Entertaining children: thankless stress.

8 Entertaining during holidays: according to researcher Thomas Holmes, the most stressful of all. In fact, he considers Christmas a stressful life event. High expectations, high expenses, and high numbers of family interactions are probably to blame.

Hidden Stress: Noise

Men suffer from noise pollution too, of course, but women often have their own special recipe for this type of hidden stress.

Mix: An alarm clock ringing, two teenagers bickering, a husband grunting, a shower running, a baby crying.

Add: A coffee pot whistling, a telephone ringing.

Blend: Pet noises, television noises, radio noises, vacuum cleaner noises, washing machine noises, clothes dryer noises.

Optional: Hair dryer drone, food processor noises, children screaming, full-house hubbub, door-slamming, toy-breaking, assorted neighbourhood noises.

Some women even find that they have a special knack for listening for noise—never mind the noises that are simply thrust upon them. They always have an ear cocked for sounds of trouble from their children, for nuances of neediness from their friends, for sounds from their babies as they breathe during the night. It's not just the noise that bothers women, it's the fact that these sounds signal special responsibilities that they generally bear alone. Noises of this nature affect concentration, irritability, and the capacity to cope.

Hidden Stress: Phobias

A phobia is an unrealistic fear or unrecognized avoidance pattern that can complicate coping and trigger female stress syndrome symptoms.

For some women, these hidden stresses are hold-overs from their childhood. Ingrid describes her phobia like this.

> I was in bed reading and enjoying the night rain. It reminded me of summers back home in Sweden. I was probably dozing because I made the first thunder-sound part of my dream. I thought I heard a car crash and sat up in bed with my heart pounding. I couldn't catch my breath or figure out whether it was night or morning. Then came the second clap of thunder and I said to myself, 'Here I go again.' All my life I have been terrified of thunder; my panic won't listen to logic. I pressed my fingers into my ears. It didn't help—I could still hear the thunder. Actually, waiting for each clap was worse than the noise itself. Thank God the storm passed quickly. When it was over, I laughed at myself; but I know the same thing will happen again and again.

For other women, phobias seem to emerge during a particular life phase and then disappear.

> Leslie had never felt any anxiety about flying until her first child was born. She didn't anticipate her fear, but found that her first flight with the baby was torture. She listened to the aeroplane engines with terror, felt dizzy every time the plane hit an air pocket, and had ominous premonitions throughout the flight. The day before their return flight she felt nauseated, chilled, and terrified. She booked a train passage to New York instead, and found that her symptoms disappeared immediately.
>
> For the next fifteen years, Leslie travelled by train or car, or chose not to travel at all. Although she knew that statistically air travel was safer than ground travel, she avoided flying at all costs.

In her late thirties, Leslie found that thinking about flying no longer made her upset. She suspects that her phobia was related to her mothering role, but cannot explain its intensity or why flying was even more stressful than the inconveniences of not flying.

For yet other women, phobias have a strong symbolic meaning, although insight alone does not seem to free them of the phobia or its stress.

Selma is a high achiever who is unreasonably afraid of heights. She cannot take a lift above the fourth floor of a building, will not look out of windows above jumping distance from the ground, and faints regularly if she must do so.

Her understanding of her phobia goes like this: 'Being a success is very important to me. I am the oldest of four sisters and I want to maintain my lead in every way. I suspect that my fear of falling is like a fear of failure—losing my footing, losing my control!

Many phobias are less obvious than the three just described, even to the phobic woman herself. A woman may go through her day avoiding situations and objects without conscious awareness. She may label herself a procrastinator, forgetful, or harried. She may suffer much inconvenience and stress and still not admit to phobic functioning.

Here are some of the most common female phobias and their possible meanings.

PHOBIA	POSSIBLE FOCUS
Fear of crowds	Loss of identity
Fear of being alone	Learned helplessness/ dependency conflicts
Fear of being criticized	Good-girl complex
Test anxiety	Fear of failure/need for achievement conflict
Fear of injections	Concern about intrusiveness
Fear of small, closed places	Fear of being trapped or powerless
Fear of mice, snakes, spiders	Fear of loss of control

Hidden Stress: Guilt

'Shoulds' and 'should nots' both trigger guilt, and guilt is a powerful hidden stressor. Women usually have very little time or opportunity to do things they 'should not' do—they struggle with 'shoulds' instead.

I should begin my diet today.

I should finish the paperwork at my office.

I should pay the bills today, but time flies.

I should have called my mother-in-law, but I dread the conversation.

I should bring the car in for a service, but what an inconvenience!

I should have gone to the PTA meeting, but they're so boring.

I should spend more time with my son, but I am so busy.

I should be more patient with my boyfriend, but he acts like a kid most of the time.

Trying to be 'good' is more frequently a source of stress for women than concern about being 'bad.' Trying to be a perfect daughter, wife, mother, employee, daughter-in-law, and friend, all at the same time, is often a female's fate. Girls are raised to be 'good.' They are praised and rewarded when they are empathetic, conforming, and considerate. Even when they enter the work world, they are expected to maintain their home responsibilities as well. Soon a pressure cooker of 'shoulds' is building up steam. Result: the female stress syndrome!

Hidden Stress: Life Events

Life events always involve stress. This is obvious if the event is an unexpected death, an unwanted divorce, or an incapacitating illness. It's less obvious if the event is a change for the good. But even good events, such as moving to a bigger house, changing to a better job, or having a long-awaited baby, can create stress by necessitating reorganization of time, energy, and expectations.

Test yourself on the Social Readjustment Scale of Life

Events, developed by Thomas Holmes and Richard Rahe. Add up the indicated points for every life event or change that you have experienced over the past year.

SOCIAL READJUSTMENT RATING SCALE[1]

Life Event	Point Value
Death of spouse	100
Divorce	73
Marital separation	65
Jail term	63
Death of close family member	63
Personal injury or illness	53
Marriage	50
Fired at work	47
Marital reconciliation	45
Retirement	45
Change in health of family member	44
Pregnancy	40
Sex difficulties	39
Gain of new family member	39
Business readjustment	39
Change in financial state	38
Death of close friend	37
Change to different line of work	36
Change in number of arguments with spouse	35
Mortgage over £15,000	31
Foreclosure of mortgage or loan	30
Change in responsibilities at work	29
Son or daughter leaving home	29
Trouble with in-laws	29
Outstanding personal achievement	28
Spouse begin or stop work	26
Begin or end school	26
Change in living conditions	25
Revision of personal habits	24
Trouble with boss	23
Change in work hours or conditions	20
Change in residence	20
Change in schools	20

Change in recreation	19
Change in church activities	19
Change in social activities	18
Mortgage or loan less than £15,000	17
Change in sleeping habits	16
Change in number of family get-togethers	15
Change in eating habits	15
Holiday	13
Christmas	12
Minor violations of the law	11

YOUR TOTAL:
Life Event   *Point Value*

[1]Thomas H. Holmes and Richard H. Rahe, 'The Social Readjustment Rating Scale,' *Journal of Psychosomatic Research* 11 (1967), pp. 213–218.

In their sample poll Holmes and Rahe found that people with scores over 300 points for one year had an 80 per cent risk of becoming seriously ill or vulnerable to depression. Those with scores between 200 and 300 points still had an impressive 50 per cent risk. Although these statistics cannot predict the risk for any particular individual, they do confirm the correlation between life-change stress and both physical and emotional health.

Now scan the Life Event Scale again. Note how many changes more frequently or more forcefully affect women than men: marriage, divorce, and reconciliation changes can totally restructure the daily life of a nonworking woman; son or daughter leaving home can trigger the 'empty nest syndrome', change in residence, recreation, church activities, social activities, family get-togethers, and the number of family members usually means more change for the wife than for the husband. Some life events are obvious, some are more subtle, but all contribute to the female stress syndrome.

An examination of divorce stresses for women points up how important life changes are to female stress.

Stress begins long before the divorce, of course. During the decision-making process, a woman must typically consider problems most men do not. If there are children, in most cases they will reside with her after the divorce. If she is a working mother, she will have to do even more juggling, since she will then be breadwinner, mother, and sometimes surrogate father. Even if there are no children involved, her life-style will be drastically changed. She will give up her homemaker status for a round of dates and all the anxiety that involves: waiting to be called, battling the numbers that tell us there are more women than men available, competing with younger women for men of all ages, and being primarily reacted to on the basis of her appearance. Or perhaps she will give up companionship altogether, depriving herself of support. Furthermore, if she looks to romance or marriage as an important component of her happiness, she must deal with all of the above while shouldering a major disappointment, the failure of her marriage, freshly experienced.

Even for those women who wanted a divorce very much, stress will be produced by the life changes involved in the break-up. Their world becomes less predictable, and their future is again full of unknowns. Frequent symptoms of divorce stress among women are difficulty in sleeping, poorer health, greater loneliness, low work efficiency, memory difficulties, increased smoking and increased drinking.

Managing the Hidden Stresses

Step one in managing hidden stresses is to *uncover* the source of the stress. Many women are victims of guilt, phobias, impatience, noise pollution, driving anxiety, and hostess hardships without realizing that each continually contributes to the female stress syndrome. Knowledge will not set you completely free, but it is a good start. The better you know yourself and your reactions to hidden stresses, the easier it will be to manage the stress and your reactions.

In most cases, a little reality-testing can go a long way. This is step two in hidden-stress management. It involves checking the old reaction against reality, and practising a new, more appropriate response. Eleanor, for example, might try giving herself permission to revise her list of 'shoulds,' and might practise saying 'It's OK' whenever she falls short of her own ideal. Selma might take herself by the hand and force herself to take the lift to the second floor of a familiar building the first week, to the third floor the next week, and so on.

Women suffering from a combination of noise pollution and a one-ear-always-listening-for-trouble syndrome may want to institute a 'time of silence' policy, or hire a sitter to be the 'listener' for an hour. Women who experience stress when they have to wait might carry a paperback novel, or a small notebook for doodling, making lists, and creative writing, or they might even practise the relaxation techniques discussed in Chapter 10 while queueing at the bank.

Driving, of course, will always be somewhat stressful, although my patients have come up with many tension-reducers. One young mother plays symphonic music in the car. She finds that it is soothing to her and to her children as well. A commuter leaves a bottle of her favourite perfume in the car, her favourite chewing gum, and a set of cassettes that teach conversational French.

Reducing life-change stresses requires using all the stress-management techniques you can muster. Since most life changes are either inevitable (such as the death of a spouse or a child leaving home) or generally irreversible (a divorce), stress management in these cases involves accepting the reality of the change. Replaying the past or pessimistically predicting a continuation in the future will not reduce stress. Addressing and dealing with the immediate present, however, will. As each step is taken, a sense of mastery and control will be gained.

NINE

Female After Forty

Today, the average forty-year-old woman can expect to live to be at least eighty years old. After the age of forty, then, many naturally start to re-examine their lives. Often they find they are as distressed as these women as they look into their future.

'I used to think forty was middle-aged. Now that I *am* forty, I wonder if I was right.'

'My mother used to tell me: You live and learn. I have noticed that we live a lot faster than we learn!'

'Time seemed to go on and on until now. I thought that I had plenty of time to find a partner or husband, even to have a family. I may have waited too long.'

'I used to think my work was everything. I no longer think *anything* is everything.'

'Now that I am no longer needed by my children, I find that I don't want to be needed by my husband either. I suppose it's part of never having been free to be myself. I went from home, to marriage, to divorce, to marriage ... without a breathing space. I don't want to divorce my husband, but I wish I had a *wife* for the next half of my life!'

'I am forty-five and still have not learned to relax. I don't know how to stop worrying about things I can't change.'

'My children have grown up; my husband has left me for a younger woman, and I am single, sixty, and sad.'

'Just when I finished parenting my children, I had to start parenting my husband's parents. When do I get to take care of myself?'

'Going through menopause was like going through a rebirth for me. I began to think of sex as pure pleasure and looked forward to planning holidays without the kids. My husband, on the other hand, became depressed when he reached middle age, and I feel as if I am living with an old man!'

'After forty, the crises never end,' according to yet another woman. Bigger children have bigger problems, and then empty the nest. Husbands retire, leave, or die. Bodies sag, spirits flag, and backaches nag. Parents die and leave their children and children's children.

Unfortunately, it is during these middle years that many women experience more anxiety and depression than at any other life stage: changing self-concepts, marriage dissatisfaction, redefinition of parenting roles, and the double standard of ageing.

The Double Standard of Ageing

In an article written more than ten years ago, Susan Sontag described the double standard of ageing in this society by comparing older women and men. How much do you think has changed since she made these observations?

● As they grow older, women often keep their age a secret. Most men do not.
● Since women are often judged on their beauty and youthfulness, their value as partners may decrease as they mature. Since men are often judged on their competence and experience, their value as partners may increase as they mature.
● As she ages, a woman's value in the job market-place often decreases, as does her pay. As a man ages, he can usually expect to be earning more than when he was younger.
● An older woman is considered less sexually attractive and desirable than a younger woman. An older man, particularly if he is financially or politically successful, does not lose his sexual eligibility. In fact, it often increases as his power increases, and the male/female mortality rates make him a scarce sexual commodity!

- Women experience menopause and, consequently, an anatomical and conceptual change of life; men may change their lives, but not through anatomical destiny.
- Older men can be expected to take younger lovers; older women are not!
- Women are expected to try to maintain facial beauty through cosmetics, moisturizers, and even surgery. Men are expected to have their faces become more rugged, scarred, and marked by the passing years.

Men and women do not approach the ageing 'starting line' neck and neck. Many of the stresses that affect women as they age have begun to form before they are forty. It is more often the woman than the man who has postponed or interrupted a career for the convenience of marriage or the necessities of parenting. It is more often the woman than the man who has assumed a submissive or compliant position when family decisions had to be made in the midst of pros and cons. It is more often the wife who is defined by her husband's status than the reverse. It is more often that a wife takes her husband's name than keeps her own— particularly among women currently over forty. It is not difficult to see the potential for stress in this sort of situation.

> Shirley flipped through the day's mail. There were eighteen envelopes. Fifteen were addressed to her husband. Two were addressed to 'Resident.' One letter was addressed to her. It was a note from her Old Girls' association asking for a contribution to a scholarship fund. She looked again at this last envelope. In fact, it was not addressed to her at all. She had attended college under the name of Shirley Green, and this letter was addressed to Mrs Richard Ashby. What has happened to Shirley Green? she wondered. She felt as though she had become somebody's mother, somebody's wife, and nobody at all to the outside world. By the time she was forty, she feared, she might disappear altogether.

Shirley did not disappear by the time she was forty. Instead, she wrote asking for her name to be listed as Shirley Green-Ashby, took over the fund-raising division of the association in order to make sure other women were similarly approached and addressed, and eventually formed a non-profit organization that helps postgraduate women establish independent companies and develop self-employed careers.

Other women, unfortunately, see less-happy endings to their struggles to cope with the double standard of ageing. Some lose their husbands to younger women. Some settle for partners they would not have chosen a decade earlier. Some withdraw from the social or occupational spheres altogether, rather than risk losing out to other women. Some buy themselves cosmetic surgery and/or younger men. Whether we are married or single, no matter what our situation, the double standard of ageing affects us and must be considered one of the special female stresses.

Re-Entry at Forty

Many women who have spent the first two decades of their adult lives in the home see themselves as 'just housewives,' though this is an inaccurate and demeaning view. They complain that they lack job qualifications, social skills, sexual experience, and personal style. By the time they are approaching forty, they would like to re-enter the world beyond their homes, but are stressed by what they consider their inadequacies.

Considering that the same activities they have performed are more valued when done by men than by women, low self-concepts among fortyish females are not surprising. Margaret Mead gives many examples of this phenomenon.

- Think of a woman cooking and you probably picture a housewife. Think of a man cooking and you picture a chef.
- Think of a woman working with clay, and you probably picture a craftsperson (or girl-scout leader, or kinder-garten teacher). Think of a man working with clay and you picture an artist.
- Think of a woman assisting a childbirth, and you probably picture a nurse or midwife. Think of a man assisting a childbirth, and you picture an obstetrician.
- Think of a woman who is assertive. She is probably

assumed to be aggressive. Think of a man who is assertive. He is assumed to be successful.

These generalizations help to explain why a woman with twenty years of homemaking experience often feels that she has little of value to offer in her later years. The reverse is true: A housewife typically has experience in accounting, nutrition, nursing, counselling, decorating, catering, social planning, and sometimes hiring, firing, and even public relations. If she has particularly enjoyed one of these areas, she can begin to focus her job or career ambitions.

In fact, the older woman is more desirable than her male counterpart both in the job market and as a mate. Research indicates that women have greater resistance to rheumatism, haemorrhages, many cancers, and brain disease. They usually have greater circulation of blood to the brain and suffer less loss of memory than men as they age. Since they retain the use of their hands, legs, and eyesight longer than men, women will remain occupationally and socially active longer.

Despite this positive report on women after forty, the myths often prevail. Husbands advise wives that they could not survive the 'dog eat dog' world of business. Men tell women that their rages, hormones, or emotional temperaments make them too illogical to function well in a man's world. Even women often view other women with prejudices, and prefer to vote for male politicians, work for male bosses, hire male employees, use male solicitors, and choose male doctors.

Sex at Sixty

The older woman is often more desirable than the older man in still another way—sexually. Although men have traditionally talked more about their sexuality, most women maintain their sexual interest and capacities far longer as they mature.

Menopause frees the older woman from any pregnancy fears she might have had, and coincides with freedom from caring for small children and from her or her husband's career struggles. Menopause can replace premenstrual tension with hot flushes and other body changes, but hot flushes pass and other changes, such as diminished vaginal lubrication, can be treated medically or compensated for. The majority of women seem to adjust well physically to menopausal changes. Why, then, do we see female stress?

The main source of sexual stress among older women is older men. Marriage itself does not insure that a sexually interested woman will have sex available in her later years.

Husbands may, for example, withdraw sexually after they have suffered a heart attack or other serious illness, even though their doctors have given them a go-ahead. The statistics on heart attacks, in fact, show a surprisingly low incidence rate of attacks during intercourse with a spouse. (It is slightly higher among men with new partners.)

Out of misguided concern, a man may also withdraw after his wife has suffered an illness.

Husbands may withdraw sexually after high blood pressure medication, diabetes, or ageing interferes with their erections.

Husbands, finally, are often older than their wives. This is financially advantageous when a couple is young, but sexually disadvantageous when a couple matures. Add to that years of familiarity, routine, and daily problems. Add anxiety about appearance and performance. Add social taboos against 'dirty old men.' The result? Wives experiencing the female stress syndrome!

Older women who are not married, or who never married, run the risk of additional problems in this area. Sexuality may be an inner quality, but sexiness, like beauty, is in the eye of the beholder. Without appreciative eyes around to behold you, it is all too easy to become lax about your exercise, diet, or appearance. Women over forty who are finding sexual partners less available should know that this is not so much a reaction against them personally, but rather the result of the double standard of ageing as well as the unfortunate imbalance in the male/female populations in this age group.

Stress and the Not-so-Merry Widow

Another source of stress in the older woman is the experience of widowhood.

When it comes to remarrying after the death of spouse, the odds are not in a woman's favour. Only one-quarter of all widows remarry within five years, compared to half of all widowers.

Sheer loneliness is one of the biggest burdens of widowhood, whether it happens at a young or older age.

Compounding loneliness are additional sources of stress that have emerged from stress workshops I have run with widows.

1 Approximately 44 per cent of widows must cope with a drop in their incomes when their spouses die. In addition, immediate funeral and other death costs are high.

2 The majority of men die without leaving a will. This precipitates lengthy and confusing legal procedures for their widows to handle.

3 Many widows can't escape the need to find an object of blame for their loss. They begin a litany of 'if-onlys' that prolongs their mourning.

4 The woman who occupied a traditional role as a housewife usually suffers a sense of confusion and helplessness when the head of the household dies and she must take over.

5 Women whose husbands were financially and socially successful find both their status and feelings of security are diminished.

6 Depression in reaction to the death is often associated with early awakening and other sleep disturbances. These, in turn, reduce the widow's coping capacity and raise the risk of female stress symptoms.

7 If the widow's spoken communication is reduced with the loss of her husband, she may gradually withdraw from social contact. Such withdrawal may become chronic, but it may not be obvious initially.

8 Many widows feel guilty if they find that they still have sexual needs. They feel disloyal to the deceased and inhibited about masturbation. Moreover, they are unlikely to find a suitable male partner.

9 Widowhood is so common that it may not rally the social-support reaction it warrants.

10 If a widow is forced by practical or financial circum-

stances to move after her husband's death, she must deal with the stresses of a significant change in routine, control, familiarity, and neighbourhood support system. If, in addition, the change is to a child's home or to an old-peoples' home, the loss of dignity and/or power and autonomy can be devastating!

Ageing in the 1980s

Although some of the stresses that beset women as they age are both universal and inevitable, others are unique to this time.

Women in the 1980s are caught in the divorce deluge. Some women over forty are leaving their husbands; some are being left. They have no models for their new life-style and no idea of what is to come. They are on the forefront of a new social world, caught in the stresses of changing expectations.

Women in the 1980s are affected by the unique economic situation, in which inflation is coupled with a recession/depression. The golden years have become tarnished as pensions and incomes fall short of today's financial needs. Women worry about their own wage-earning capacities; about their retirement plans; about their security should they remain unmarried, or should their husbands die or leave, about their independence in their later years; and about their children's economic survival.

Women in the 1980s are concerned about their daughters. Just as the lives of women over forty are radically different from the lives their mothers led, so are their own grown daughters' lives different. Their daughters are marrying later, working more, having fewer children, and divorcing more quickly. Today's women over forty do not escape the female stress syndrome.

Managing After-Forty Stress

Menopause
Menopause, of course, is biologically programmed (unless surgery precipitates it), and the physical changes it brings are not totally under your control. But you can reduce the stress of feeling helpless and victimized by Mother Nature.

88

Although the menopause symptoms themselves may not be under your control, other areas of functioning are:

- Maintain control of your weight, following a nutritionally sound diet, and you will continue to enjoy your body.
- Set up and follow an exercise programme. This will maintain your muscle strength and stimulate your energy supply.
- Schedule your time. Decide on your own priorities and handle time as if it were a very valuable commodity.
- Be good to yourself. This can help to reduce that feeling of being controlled by physical changes rather than your own decisions. Treat yourself well: take bubble baths, read good books, eat delicious, nutritional food.
- Take notice of your needs and be ready to *ask* for what may be needed from others: sympathy, support, closeness, distance, respect, or attention.

If the physical symptoms or stress symptoms seem excessive, consult your doctor. If you have a hard time deciding whether or not the symptoms are excessive, ask that very question.

As previously mentioned, there is a very positive side to menopause. Many women experience it as a relief, even as a rebirth. They find freedom from fear of pregnancy that is liberating both sexually and practically, free from premenstrual tensions and postnatal blues. With menopause often comes a re-examination of goals and roles. Here at last is the opportunity to make resolves and choose courses of action that had been postponed, or not even considered. There are many women like Lena, who never considered that the years after mothering would be any less full or important, and planned for them.

Lena, began to plan for her eventual retirement from mothering when she was only thirty-eight. She started by enrolling in a counselling programme that had evening classes, and by the time she reached menopause she had received her master's degree in social work. She had also completed her full-time mothering responsibilities. She is pleased with the way she pursued her interests sequentially, rather than trying to juggle them simultaneously.

Managing the Stress of Grief

Although, of course, there are individual differences, widows may find comfort in the fact that grief and mourning often have distinct, predictable stages. Each is a necessary step in the natural healing process.

Phase I: 'If I deny it, it's not true' The widow will try to avoid any thought or mention of the loss in an attempt to escape pain. Some will act as if nothing had happened, for a while. They will attend to business and continue their work. Others will withdraw from friends and family to avoid mention or association with memories of the deceased. Still others seem to be numb and unfeeling.

Phase II: 'I have the power to undo it' During this stage, many widows may try to escape the sadness of acceptance by utilizing mystical thinking. Attempts to keep the spouse alive by 'seeing' and 'hearing' him are not uncommon, nor are beliefs that he is still right here on earth in spirit, to be communicated with.

Phase III: 'I can't do anything about it' The loss is faced and felt during this difficult period. The reality of the death of the spouse can lead to despair and even suicidal notions. The turning point will be not the acceptance of helplessness with regard to her husband's death, but power and control with regard to the widow's own *life*. As she makes choices and reshapes her life, re-engagement will begin.

Phase IV: 'I am rebuilding, and every now and then I remember' In my clinical experience, I have noticed one common characteristic: the widow's healthy sense of surprise that she has been able to manage her loss and grief, and often to feel stronger for it. Widows realize that they were not merely half of a pair, but are, in fact, a whole person in their own right. Many choose to remain on their own and enjoy the control they have over their lives.

Living Alone and Liking It

If your marriage or long-term relationship ends, or you have difficulty adjusting to the fact of being forty-plus and on your own, there are a number of steps you can take to make the experience more positive.

First of all, don't *judge* your needs. Help yourself go after what you need to feel good without harsh self-judgments.

Turn to your family and friends. This is not a sign of weakness, not a lack of self-sufficiency. You're not the only one who needs to be needed.

Don't try to run away from intermittent sadness or loneliness. If you repress these feelings, the same repressive system will likely put the lid on *all* strong feelings—including joy and humour as well.

If a long-term relationship has just ended for whatever reason, accept the fact that you have gone through a transition and that any change, particularly one over which you have little or no control, will aggravate the symptoms of the female stress syndrome. You may be more prone to depression or illness, depending on your 'weak links.' You may feel social stresses more, be more sensitive to insults and injuries from others. Remember that the female stress syndrome is real—it's not all in your mind. Help yourself and be good to yourself.

If you have recently been widowed, be aware that guilt is a common side effect: guilt that you are still alive while your spouse is not, guilt that from time to time you felt anger toward him when he was alive, guilt that you may even be enjoying some aspects of your widowhood, guilt that feelings for another man may be developing.

Also, especially at first, take as much time as you can to make big decisions (such as whether or not to sell the house, where you should live if you do). If possible, don't let yourself be pressured into something before you're ready; in the midst of grief and coming to terms with a major life change, it is difficult to think clearly, and you may make decisions you will later regret.

Develop a network of people who share the same problems and feelings; you'll feel less alone. Fight some of the injustices of age prejudice, if that is your style. It will make you feel more potent. Keep in mind that as your sense of control increases, your stress decreases, so anything you can do to put yourself more in control of your life will go a long way toward easing the female stress syndrome.

TEN

Living with Female Stress

Up until now we have been examining the stresses that make up the female stress syndrome, and the symptoms associated with those stresses. We have seen how the stresses that stem from a woman's biology and conditioning can trigger a wealth of physical and psychological ailments that, to one degree or another, are a fact of life for most of us. Now it is time to focus on *living with* the female stress syndrome.

The aim of female stress syndrome management is threefold. The first aim is to increase a sense of control. The higher one's sense of control, the lower one's stress.

The second aim of female stress syndrome management is to encourage realistic assessment of the stressful situation. Some stressful situations are short-term and require minor management efforts. Others are long-term and chronic—more likely to put women at high risk for stress symptoms, and requiring major stress-management efforts. Realistic assessment will help determine which are best handled through *action*, and which are best handled through *acceptance*.

The third aim of female stress syndrome management is to improve problem-solving skills and coping strategies. Every encounter with the female stress syndrome should leave a woman better equipped to deal with stress when it next appears.

Helping Yourself

Always remember, as I said at the outset of this book, that *you are entitled to try to reduce the stress in your life*. Give yourself permission to take control over your life, to stop feeling guilty, to worry less about the 'shoulds' that inevitably crop up.

Separate Your Past from Your Present
Don't re-create old scenarios again and again with the new people in your life. They will not change in the reliving. They will not give you mastery over the past. Instead, address the present: it is the present over which you can really take control.

Don't assume the future will be the same as the past.

Accept Yourself as a Package Deal
You cannot be perfect. Don't even try. Replace 'This is who I should be' with 'This is who I seem to be.' Work with your reality, not your ideal.

Break the Habit of Living Life Laced with Guilt
When we are young, most of our guilt follows behaviour that we learned was *bad*. When we are adults, however, we have little time or impulse to be 'bad.' More often, our guilt follows behaviour that falls short of what we learned was *good*. Women say to themselves 'I should have . . .' all day long.

'I should have said yes . . .'
'I should have said no . . .'
'I should have called . . .'
'I should have offered . . .'

This type of guilt serves no purpose except to increase stress.

Learn to Say No

- Learn to say no without feeling guilt (as to a child).
- Learn to say no without justifying yourself (as to your spouse).
- Learn to say no without defending yourself (as to a parent).
- Learn to say no graciously, not tentatively (as to your lover).
- Learn to give explanations, not excuses (as to the boss).

Give Yourself the Freedom to Change Your Mind
Don't persecute yourself every time you change your mind

about something or someone. Reassessing is a mark of flexibility, not instability.

Become Your Own Permission-Giver
You don't need permission from others to take care of yourself, to reduce your own stress level. Don't wait until the whole world can see that you are under stress before you allow yourself a rest. Don't wait until you feel you can't cope with one more problem before you start to take care of yourself. If you wait for others to take care of you, you might wait forever.

- Rest: take a nap, a bath, or whatever—you're entitled!
- Relax: read a book, watch television, write a poem, listen to music, nap—and don't *contaminate* this relaxation time with chores.
- Set realistic limits: underwhelm yourself, underschedule yourself, and underdemand.

Become Your Own Best Friend
Be on the lookout for stressors that trigger your stress symptoms. Protect yourself as you would your other loved ones.

Become Your Own Resource Person
Learn how to manage *emergencies* that are inevitable or highly probable: funeral arrangements, medical crises, car problems. Compile lists of hot lines, professionals, and references.

Learn how to manage your reactions to those *situational stresses* that particularly affect you: holidays, in-law problems, or financial worries. Don't be caught upset; anticipate and alleviate your reactions.

Become Your Own Catharsis Expert
For short-term or emergency stress, catharsis techniques can help you cope. Catharsis is the emotional equivalent of a pressure cooker blowing off some of its steam through the lid valve. If the valve becomes stuck and the pressure builds to the point of eruption—pot roast on the ceiling! Catharsis techniques aim at discharging the tension that accumulates during stressful situations. They increase our

sense of control by giving us the means to moderate our pressure levels, vital during times of stress. They exercise and relax our bodies, make good use of the extra adrenaline produced during stress, and direct 'nervous' energy. They provide a healthy distraction from our immediate stress.

Some cathartic activities are self-regulated and self-contained. They don't require a partner or equipment. They include

- Walking—the most common exercise for both men and women of all ages.
- Exercise—work out at home or at health clubs.
- Swimming—very relaxing.
- Jogging—fast becoming the most popular stress antidote!

Other cathartic activities are competitive. They include

- Tennis
- Team sports
- Marathons
- Games (backgammon, cards)

Become Your Own Relaxation Expert
Counteract tension with a soothing environment. Warm baths, hot tubs, long showers, Jacuzzis, whirlpools, saunas, and Turkish baths all work for some women. An hour in a library, museum, gallery, bookstore, or favourite chair with a book or music help others.

Use autohypnosis to let your body know that this is its time to relax. The simple steps for entering and exiting from autohypnosis are as follows.

1 Sit comfortably in a chair facing a wall about eight feet away. Pick a spot or an object on the wall that is about one foot above your sitting eye level. This is your focal point.
2 Look at your focal point, and begin counting backward from 100, one number for each breath you exhale.
3 As you count and continue to concentrate on your focal point, imagine yourself floating, floating down, down through the chair, very relaxed.

4 As you stare at your focal point you will find that your eyelids feel heavier and begin to blink. When this happens, just let your eyes slowly close.

5 While your eyes are closed continue to count backward, one number for each time you exhale. As you count, imagine how it would feel to be as limp as a rag doll, totally relaxed and floating in a safe, comfortable space.

6 As that safe, comfortable feeling flows over you, stop counting and just float.

7 If any disturbing thought enters your space, just let it flow out again; continue to feel safe and relaxed.

8 When you're ready to come out of autohypnosis, either let yourself drift off to sleep, or count from one to three and exit using the following steps. At *one*, let yourself get ready; at *two*, take a deep breath and hold it for a few seconds; and at *three* exhale and open your eyes slowly. As you open your eyes, continue to hold on to that relaxed, comfortable feeling.

You can also counteract tension with progressive relaxation. Some of my patients make a tape of their own voice issuing the following instructions:

1 Starting with your toes, relax them.
2 Then the feet and ankles: relax.
3 Then the calves: relax.
4 The knees: relax.
5 The thighs: relax.
6 The buttocks: relax.
7 The abdomen and stomach: relax.
8 The back and shoulders: relax.
9 The hands: relax.
10 The forearms: relax.
11 The upper arms: relax.
12 The neck: relax.
13 The face: relax.
14 Drift off.

Finally, try counteracting tension with the following technique. You will first slowly contract and relax each part of your body for ten seconds each; and then contract and relax each part of your body more quickly to become aware of the tension-relaxation contrast.

1 Frown as hard as you can for ten seconds; then relax those forehead muscles for ten seconds. Now repeat this more quickly, frowning and relaxing for one second each and becoming aware of the different feelings of each movement.

2 Squeeze your eyes shut for ten seconds, then relax for ten seconds. Repeat quickly.

3 Wrinkle your nose hard for ten seconds; then relax for ten seconds. Repeat quickly.

4 Slowly press your lips together; then relax. Repeat quickly.

5 Press your head back against the wall, floor, or bed (real or imaginary)—then relax. Repeat quickly.

6 Bring your left shoulder up in a tight shrugging motion; relax. Repeat quickly.

7 Do the same with your right shoulder; repeat quickly.

8 Press your straightened arms back against the wall, or floor, or bed; relax. Repeat quickly.

9 Clench your fists tightly for ten seconds. Relax your hands and let the tension flow out through your fingers. Repeat quickly.

10 Contract your chest cavity for ten seconds and release. Repeat quickly.

11 Press your back against the wall or floor; relax. Repeat quickly.

12 Tighten your buttock muscles for ten seconds; relax. Repeat quickly.

13 Press your straightened legs against the wall or floor or bed; relax. Repeat quickly.

14 Slowly flex your feet, stretching your toes as far back toward you as possible; relax and let tension flow out through your toes. Repeat quickly.

15 Check for tense spots and repeat the exercise where you find any.

Soon you will begin to recognize muscle contractions caused by tension before these contractions can cause spasms and chronic pain.

Create Self-Fulfilling Prophecies

Expect the best. Even if things do not work out the way you might have wanted them to, at least you have not stressed yourself *before* the problem or disappointment.

Use the 'as if' technique. That is, behave *as if* everyone would be delighted to treat you just the way you want to be treated.

Ellen was trying to attend evening classes and run a three-child household at the same time. She needed her husband's moral support, financial aid, and household help. She was feeling that she wasn't entitled to them, however. 'Going to college is so self-indulgent,' she thought. 'I really should be working part time, rather than studying part time,' she chided herself. Although her husband had not said a word against her studies, she was always prepared for his criticism. She read things into his remarks, became defensive if he was tired, and felt angry if he wanted her time. She put herself under so much pressure with this anticipatory anxiety that she was ready to quit classes.

As a last resort, Ellen decided to try the 'as if' technique. She gave herself permission to be a part-time student and began to behave as if she believed it was fine with her husband, too. Now she was able to react to his helpfulness with appreciation rather than guilt, and she never let an opportunity go by to praise his support in front of friends.

In Ellen's case, the 'as if' assumption was closer to reality than her own pessimistic assumptions. Her husband increased his efforts to be helpful and understanding, and she felt less stressed.

The 'as if' technique:

- Facilitates asking for favours without a trace of defensiveness.
- 'Teaches' others that we see ourselves as worth positive treatment and entitled to consideration.
- Flatters others by making *requests* of them—not demands.
- Reinforces reactions in others that will reduce, rather than increase, stress.

Enjoy Your Own Sexuality

If you have a sexual partner, don't neglect the sexual side of yourself when you are under stress. For many women, sexual activity is an important outlet for tension. It helps women remember that they are desirable, attractive, needed, or wanted. And by being intimate, they close out the rest of the world temporarily, providing a vital respite from stress.

Stay Self-Centred

By self-centred I do not mean selfish; I mean self-aware. Remind yourself continually to look at yourself and at the world through your *own* eyes, not through others' eyes.

Do not constantly view yourself through others' eyes and change your opinion of yourself and of your decisions, even when important people in your life disagree. Don't re-evaluate yourself every time your partner, children, or friends disapprove. Don't give others the power to knock you off balance.

Assess Your Stress

You cannot manage stressors or symptoms until you can identify them. With pencil in hand, review the list of stress symptoms below. Add others in the blanks provided. During the course of a day, note the time when you experienced any symptom on the list. Next to the time, jot down the activity you were engaged in or about to begin. Do you find a pattern?

TIME	ACTIVITY	SYMPTOM
		Headache
		Heartburn
		Nausea
		Cold sweat
		Dizziness
		Memory block
		Asthma

TIME	ACTIVITY	SYMPTOM
		Hyperventilation
		Allergic reaction
		Backache
		Swallowing difficulty
		Rapid heartbeat
		Increased blood pressure
		Urinary frequency

If you find that certain activities seem to trigger stress symptoms for you, deal with them in the following ways:

1 Assess the timing of the activity. Could you do the task earlier or later in the day? Would this make a difference in terms of stress?
2 Assess your performance level. Are you over-invested in this activity? Are you spending too much time and energy in this area?
3 Assess your motivation. Are you letting a sense of 'should' dictate your behaviour? Too often an activity we might enjoy is resented because we feel compelled rather than motivated to complete it.

Anticipate the Stress of Holidays
Holidays involve a change in schedule, a gathering of family, and high expectations—usually too high! For many, they evoke upsetting memories of good times lost or bad times past. For some, they emphasize feelings of being alone and isolated. And most people find that holidays require extraordinary preparation, work, and cleaning up.

Take holidays one moment at a time. Some moments will be memorable; some will be disappointing. Enjoy what each *does* bring: food, a break from work, visual beauty, religious

100

feelings. Try not to compare a holiday experience with those past, or with those to come.

Aim for Self-Management, Not Quick Change

Your personality structure was years and years in the making. Your earliest years constituted your introduction to 'reality.' Because those years preceded speech, they are not even accessible through your memory. Think back to your earliest memory. Chances are you are thinking about something that happened when you were two or three years old. Your sense of safety, security, and self had long since begun to form. Think back to your junior school. Can you remember every teacher you had? No? And yet you spent a *year* with each!

Most stress reduction can be more quickly and realistically achieved by *knowing* your personality structure than by changing it. Work *with* your defences, strengths, and weaknesses, not against them. Self-deprecation increases stress; self-management does not. Unrealistic attempts at personality change are frustrating and increase stress. Self-acceptance does not.

Move Into the Here and Now

Many women increase their stress by being so pulled into reliving past problems and so pushed into 'preliving' future fears that they are rarely living in the 'here and now.' Life is literally passing them by, and so are opportunities for quiet moments, little pleasures, and deep breaths. If this is one of your problems, continually bring yourself back from upsetting hypothetical scenarios into the present, and try to live life as an ongoing process, not a series of upcoming crises.

Practice, Practice, Practice

Therapists have learned that insight is usually not enough to change behaviour. What is needed after insight is practice, practice, practice. Practising new behaviours leads to new types of reactions from others, new information about alternatives, and new views of realities. Start practising now.

When you are under stress, practise *acting*, not reacting.

1 Help yourself do this by taking the time to collect information about a situation or person before you draw conclusions. If someone's behaviour is upsetting, don't take it personally. Process what you are seeing and feeling as information, not insult. Decide how *you* feel about what they are saying or doing, and what their behaviour says about them.
2 Help yourself do this by determining the logical consequences of the situation or of someone's behaviour, not by dwelling on illogical 'what ifs,' or 'This must mean that . . .'
3 Help yourself by *not* giving others the power to make you react before you are ready.
4 Help yourself by recognizing when you are backing off from a goal because of fear of failure, rather than moving forward towards it. Walk right up to your goals; don't back off.

Laugh, Laugh, Laugh
Laughter is the signal for the female stress syndrome centres to turn off the emergency adaptation system. It defuses tension when an embarrassing topic has come up in a joke, when an unacceptable thought or impulse has been spoken out loud, or when a perspective has been changed or regained. It lights up our faces, relaxes our muscles, lowers our sense of vigilance, restores our objectivity, and enhances hope.

Pursue Both Short-Term and Long-Term Remedies
As you begin to develop your own stress-management programme, keep in mind that you will need continually to pursue both short-term *and* long-term remedies. Exercise, autohypnosis, relaxation techniques, sex, and even laughter are short-term remedies that will help you feel more comfortable with your body and more positive about yourself. They provide immediate gratification and release. Long-term solutions, including the various aspects of behaviour modification discussed in this chapter—learning to live in the present rather than in the past, learning to feel less guilt, accepting what you cannot change about your life, giving yourself permission to take time off and reduce

stress—will increase your sense of control and help reduce chronic stress. Both kinds of techniques are vital to counteracting the stress in your life.

The stresses that plague women are a part of our lives; so too are its symptoms. We cannot ignore them, feel guilty about them, or let them overwhelm us. Recognizing the effect they have on us means that we will no longer need to turn to others for an incomplete explanation of what is going on. Learning how to manage them means we will no longer need to settle for the recommendation that we simply get a good night's sleep—or take two Valium. Female stress must be taken seriously—by women, their families, and their friends. It must be countered with understanding, self-help, and, where appropriate, with professional help.

Turn your hand palm-up and look at what is called your lifeline—the line that starts between the thumb and first finger and curves around the base of the thumb almost to the wrist. Your lifeline has a beginning, a middle, and an end. It does not go on forever. Life, too, has a beginning, a middle, and an end; it, too, does not go on forever. From now on, whenever you look at your hand, be reminded that the time to reduce stress is *now*! Don't wait until stress symptoms overwhelm your capacity for work or play. Don't wait until your doctor, family, or friends beg you to start taking care of yourself.

I began this book with a quotation 'Complete freedom from stress is death.' Contrary to public opinion, he points out, we cannot avoid stress. We are in fact *surrounded* by stress, especially where money, work, family, children, and sex are concerned. We experience stresses connected with our physiology and our daily routines, stresses that crop up at holidays. Short-term stress can help us achieve what we want to achieve. Long-term stress can help us mature—but only if we gain control over it where possible and, where it is beyond our control, try to manage the effects it has on us. More than ever, it is vitally important that we learn how to live with stress, so that we can really enjoy the full, healthy lives we were meant to have.

Bibliography

Budoff, Penny Wise, *No More Hot Flashes and Other Good News*, G. P. Putnam's Sons, New York, 1983.

Caine, Lynn, *Widow*, Bantam Books, New York, 1975.

Cousins, Norman, *Anatomy of an Illness as Perceived by the Patient*, W. W. Norton, New York, 1979.

Dalton, Katharina, *The Premenstrual Syndrome*, Heinemann, London, 1964.

Friedman, Meyer, 'Type A Behavior: A Progress Report', *The Sciences* 20 (2), 1980.

Friedman, Meyer, and Rosenman, Ray, *Type A Behavior and Your Heart*, Alfred A. Knopf, New York, 1974.

Holmes, T. H., and Rahe, R. H. 'The Social Readjustment Rating Scale', *Journal of Psychosomatic Research* 11, 1967: 213–218.

McKinlay, S., and Jeffreys, M., 'The Menstrual Syndrome', *British Journal of Preventive and Social Medicine* 28 (2), 1974: 108.

Money, John, and Ehrhardt, Anke A., *Man and Woman: Boy and Girl*, Johns Hopkins University Press, Baltimore, 1972.

Rees, L., 'Premenstrual Tension Syndrome and Its Treatment', *British Medical Journal* 1, 1953: 1014–1016.

Selye, Hans, *The Stress of Life*, rev. ed., McGraw-Hill, New York, 1976.

Selye, Hans, *Stress without Distress*, Signet, New York, 1974.

Williams, Juanita H., *Psychology of Women*, W. W. Norton, New York, 1977.

Index

Achievement, need for 38–9
Aggression 36, 38, 49–50
    control 6
Ageing 20–1, 81–91 *see also Menopause*
Alcoholism 25–6
Ambivalence 39
Amenorrhoea 28–9
Anger 62
Anorexia nervosa 22–4, 28
Anticipation, and stress 98, 100
Antiprostaglandins 15
Anxiety 13, 33–4, 38
    anticipatory 98, 100
Appetite 59

Bacon, M. 37
Barry, H. 37
Behaviour change 101–2
Bereavement 90–1
Birth control 62
Blood sugar 9
Bonding 51, 53
Bone metabolism 20
Brain chemicals 14
Breathing patterns 9
Bulimia 24–5

Careers, effect of stress on 66–9
  see also Employment
Catharsis 94–5
Child, I. L. 37
Childbirth, and premenstrual tension
    13–14
Clothes, buying 68
Competition 68
Cramps, premenstrual 15
Crises, life 4, 76–9, 86–7, 90–1

Dalton, Katharina 13
Death, coping with 86–8, 90–1
Dependency 49
Depression 21, 78
Diet 69, 78
Digestion 9
Displacement 49
Divorce 63, 78–9, 88

Driving, as stressor 71–2, 80

Economics 88, 62
Emergencies 94
Employment 88
    benefits 69–70
    re-entry 84
    tips on 68–9
Endocrine system 9
Entertaining, as stressor 72–3
Executive stress 67
Exercise, cathartic 94–7
Expectations 45

Failure, fear of 39–40
Fight, flight, or fright system 8, 34
Freud, Sigmund 34
Friedan, Betty 51
Friedman, Meyer 67
Frigidity 30–1
Frustration, sexual 51

General Adaptation Syndrome 7
Guilt 76, 93

Headaches 13, 27
Heart, stress-related problems 7
Holmes, Thomas 77, 78
Housework 54, 68–9
Hyperventilation 9

Illness, stress-related 10
Infertility 33
Intellectual stimulation 70

Job discrimination 66
Jobs *see* Employment; Mothers, working

Laughter 102
List-making 69
Living alone 90
Loneliness, in widowhood 87–8
Love, 'symptoms' 42

Maccoby, Eleanor 84–5
Manipulation tactics 46–8

Marriage 43-6
   'Dutch treat' 63
Mead, Margaret 84-5
Menopausal melancholia 21
Menopause 19-21, 86, 88-9
   and physical fitness 21
Menstruation 29-30
   see also Premenstrual tension
Migraine headache 9, 27
Mood changes 15
Motherhood
   managing 60-1
   role stress 57-60
   and sexuality 51-2
Mother's Stress Checklist 58-60
Mothers, working 55-7, 64-5
Muscle co-ordination 7

Nervous system, response to stress 8-9
Noise, as stressor 73-4
Nonassertiveness training 36-40
   retraining 41

Oestrogen 13-14, 20
Orgasmic dysfunction 32
Outlook 59

Panic attacks 34
Passivity 50
Perfectionism 67
Performance anxiety 51
Perls, Fritz 44
Phobias 74-5
Postnatal depression 18-19
Pregnancy, stress risks 16-18
Premenstrual tension 12-15
   symptoms 12-15
   treatment 15
Premotherhood 29-32
Progesterone 14, 20
Projection 48-9
Prolactin 15

Rahe, Richard 77, 78
Reaction 44
Reassurance 70
Regression, in marriage 43
Relationship stress 48-50
   management 52-3

Relaxation 68, 95-7
Role models 46
Rosenman, Ray 67

Salt intake 15
Second Stage, The (Friedan) 51
Self-acceptance 93-5
Self-hypnosis 69
Self-knowledge 58-9, 99, 101
Selye, Hans 1
Sexism 66
Sex therapy 51
Sexual fears 51
Sexuality 50-1, 99
   after menopause 85-6
Sexual repression 32
Sexual stereotypes 37-8
Sexual withdrawal 50
Singles 39-40
Sleep 59
Social life, and working 69-70
Social readjustment, scale of life
   events 77-9
Sontag, Susan 82-3
Stress
   assessment 99-100
   effects 2, 8-11
   management 79-80, 92-7
   origins 4-5
   premenstrual 15
Success, fear of 66
Support systems 54-5
Sympathy 70

Temper control 38
Tension relief 68, 95-7
Touch 6
Tranquillizers 15
Type A behaviour 66-70

Ulcers

Vaginismus 31-2
Violence, premenstrual 13
Vitamin B_6 15
Vulnerability 46-7

Waiting, as stressor 72
Water retention 14, 15
Widowhood 86-8